MW00768519

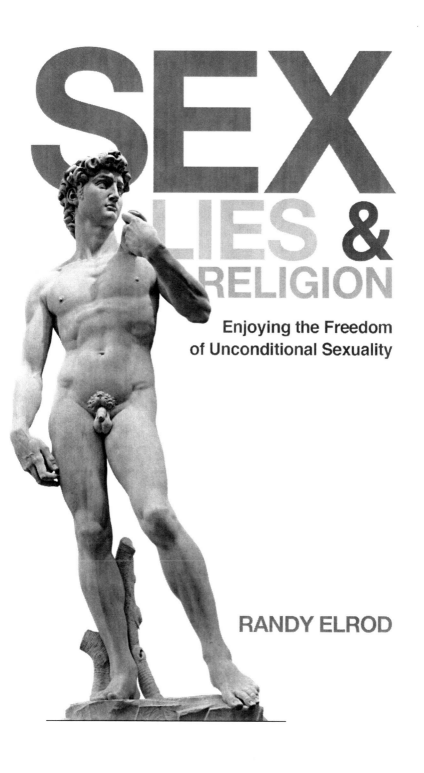

SEX
LIES &
RELIGION

**Enjoying the Freedom
of Unconditional Sexuality**

RANDY ELROD

contact randy

To Book Randy For Speaking, Call

(800) 425-0873

For More Information, go to

www.SexLiesAndReligion.com

Cover design and layout by GradientOverlay.com | Cover photo istockphoto.com

Scripture taken from The Message. Copyright © 1993, 1994, 1995, 1996, 2000, 2001, 2002. Used by permission of NavPress Publishing Group.

Scripture taken from the HOLY BIBLE, NEW INTERNATIONAL VERSION®. Copyright © 1973, 1978, 1984 Biblica. Used by permission of Zondervan. All rights reserved.

Library of Congress Control Number: 2010900033
Printed in the United States of America
ISBN # 978-0-615-34605-2

cre:ate2.0
PUBLISHING
Franklin / Tennessee / 2010

contents

To Chris,

My lover and my best friend.
Thanks for showing me how
to know love
and how to see God.

introduction

One of the most romantic times of my life was spent on a deserted island off the coast of Georgia. Miraculously spared the effects of man, the island remains essentially as it was created—a déjà vu remembrance of Eden's beauty. Narrow beams of sunlight pierced the dense canopy of virgin trees laced seductively with Spanish moss, illuminating motes of sand like dancing jewels.

A narrow road of sand over two hundred years old twisted and turned through a vast primordial jungle, ending in miles of mountainous sand dunes that gleamed pure white against a cerulean blue sky. Climbing the final dune, a sudden involuntary loss of breath occurred upon spying the untouched beach that stretched endlessly for miles in either direction. The undulating surf sparkled like diamonds.

My childhood sweetheart and wife of thirty years stood beside me. We dared not speak for fear of breaking the spell of this once-in-a-lifetime magical adventure together. Suddenly, like uninhibited children, we half-slid, half-ran down the dune, doffing shoes and clothes as we raced gleefully to the emerald water, romping and splashing for hours. As we played, feral horses grazed nearby and even a solitary alligator quietly roamed the beach. It was a thoroughly wild, surreal and originary experience.

Later as we walked the beach, naked and unashamed, we realized this must have been what Adam and Eve felt as they explored the delights of a new world together—lovers created just as God intended. We succumbed to the experience and laid a very modern towel on the soft, warm beach and in the bright sunlight of a perfect day, gently and lovingly began to act more like the adults we are.

For those of us from a religious background, it seems difficult, if not impossible, to view our experiences with God in sensual terms like the story just recounted. Unfortunately, religious lies have programmed the ability to embrace God as Lover right out of our souls—and bodies.

So, the question I dare to pose is this: Have you ever had an experience with God that was so amazing it exceeded your wildest and most fulfilling sexual moment? If the answer is no, you are not alone. Out of the hundreds of people I have asked this question, only one has said yes.

It is my hope in *Sex, Lies, and Religion* to offer a careful and thoughtful approach and application of scripture that will provide you the opportunity to experience profound intimacy with a seemingly untouchable and unseeable God. When we embrace these truths, we also discover God's original plan for our sexuality.

When I escape to the privacy of a romantic place to make passionate love with my earthly lover, much as Solomon erotically describes in scripture's Song of Songs, I somehow transcend time and space. Playful foreplay, soft whispers, and gentle caresses combine with candles, incense, and songs of love and lead to a gradual and then explosive climax. Time ceases to exist as this sexual experience provides opportunity for a total communion of both body and soul.

The next moments give way to what psychologists call the "afterglow." Dr. J. Harold Ellens describes the afterglow as those few precious moments when, no matter how bad your financial situation, how stressful your family life, or what is going wrong in the world, for a few brief minutes all seems right with the world.

Now, compare that to what I recently experienced attending the Festival Eucharist of Easter Day at a local Episcopal Church. I escaped to the privacy of a sacred, and yes, romantic place. Soft music played, beginning a joyful "foreplay," if you will, of poems, genuflections, and soft whispers called prayers. Candles, incense, and songs of love enhanced the gradual, upward path to the celebration of Holy Communion.

Every moment of the liturgy led to a climax in which I received into my body and soul the bread and wine—the body and blood of Jesus Christ. Through the liturgy, I stepped into timelessness. A surreal, multi-sensual transcendence of time and space took place in this mystery called Communion.

During this ecstatic and climactic intercourse of body and soul, the lyrics and music of Beethoven's "Ode to Joy" soared:

> *Joyful, joyful, we adore Thee,*
> *God of glory, Lord of love;*
> *Hearts unfold like flowers before thee,*
> *Opening to the Son above.*
> *Melt the clouds of sin and sadness,*
> *Drive the dark of doubt away;*
> *Giver of immortal gladness,*
> *Fill us with the light of day.*

The next moments were mysteriously reminiscent of the afterglow experienced after a sexual encounter with a lover. All seemed right with the world.

Is it possible that there is a real parallel here, established by an invisible God to help us touch and see Him?

I believe that unlearning sexual lies makes it possible to enjoy guilt-free sexual pleasure, even as it allows you to experience God more deeply. I believe that understanding the beauty and sexual symbolism of Holy Communion and embracing sexual and spiritual redemption enables you to bring all of who you are both to the sexual and the spiritual experience. I challenge you to let Sacred Consummation deepen your passion and intimacy.

Life is a mystery,
everyone must stand alone.
I hear you call my name
And it feels like home.[1]

part I. religion

1.

where soul meets body

"I want to live where soul meets body, and let the sun wrap its arms around me, and bathe my skin in water cool and cleansing, and feel, feel what its like to be new."
Death Cab for Cutie

A monk dipped his cloak into the decaying flesh of a dead woman, so the smell might banish fantasies about her. A young nun slept on a hard floor covered in ashes to tame her body when the flow of her periods first began. A monk in training prudently wrapped his hands in his cloak as he carried his elderly mother across a stream because he was taught the flesh of all women is fire.[1] Monks attempted barbarous and bloody self-castration in their cells to banish evil desires that continually "defiled" their purity. Women who took the vows of a virgin were assured the very heights of heaven, but if those vows were renounced, they were relegated to the very deepest pits of hell.[2]

In places, the early Christian record reads more carnal than a psycho-sexual horror movie. Granted, these are extreme examples that I've cited, but even if we allow for that fact, we have to ask, what sort of ideological backdrop would give rise to these particular extremities?

In this book I will make the case that early Christian views of human sexuality are very different from the biblical view. I will further make the case that these traditional misconceptions (in some cases, even heresies) still affect the thinking of Christians today. The result is a lot of screwed-up thinking about sex, ranging from a prudish suspicion (even outright hatred) of sexuality on the one hand, to rampant immorality—even among professing Christians—on the other. Both extremes are born of an unbiblical dichotomy between a pure soul and a sinful body.

The prude deals with this false rupture by subordinating the flesh; the libertine deals with it by pretending that the spirit has nothing to say to the flesh. Either person is in bondage. People (especially religious people) feel isolated and alone when dealing with sexual issues. Shedding light on misunderstanding and lies can lead to a life of freedom not plagued by unnecessary guilt. Surprisingly, the freedom to enjoy a spiritually sexual life is far less limited than religion would have us think.

Perhaps the most depressing thing about this wrongheadedness about sex is the fact that it closes off one of the most important paths by which God reveals Himself to us. God is our great Lover, pursuing us out of an ardent desire—a desire that we reciprocate when we are spiritually healthy. As we come to terms with God's unconditional love for us, we experience a sexual freedom that is rarely experienced by modern-day believers. And as we experience that freedom as complete spiritual and sexual beings, we become fully alive.

Ironically, among the ancients, the pagans were often more "biblical" than the early Christians. Call it common grace, or maybe a lucky guess, but the pagan understanding of sex as a meeting place between the fleshly and the eternal comes closer to God's truth than the false dichotomy between flesh and spirit. After all, I'm talking about a God who Himself took on flesh to draw near to us.

I don't want to paint with too broad a brush here either: "pagans" believed a lot of different things about sex, some of them as wrong as they could possibly be. And there were early Christians who fought valiantly against the separation of flesh and spirit. Nevertheless, we would do well to consider what was good and healthy in the pagan traditions that celebrated sex as a vital part of life, including the spiritual life.

The Lie of Sexual Renunciation

When it comes to sexuality, somehow self-denial came to be treated as the highest, holiest good in Christian circles. I call it the lie of sexual renunciation—the idea that a celibate life is holier than a married life, and that if you're married, less sex with your spouse is holier than more sex. We realize that, properly speaking, this is not the "orthodox" view of the Church. But haven't you felt this attitude as an undercurrent—perhaps unspoken—of church culture? Orthodox or not, the lie of renunciation has affected Christians' attitudes toward sex, and it is worth examining.

To "renounce" is to disclaim or to disown. To renounce one's son or daughter is to say, "You are no longer my child. Don't expect to receive an inheritance, and don't expect me to fulfill any of my other parental obligations either." To renounce your sexuality is to say, in effect, "This doesn't belong to me. This sexual nature has caused me trouble and heartache, but it's not really me; the 'real' me is the soul that finds itself stuck in this body. I don't owe one thing to that bodily, sexual part of me."

Early Christians mistrusted the body in ways that still affect our attitudes today. Consider, for instance, the Desert Fathers of the third century A.D. They fled the cities and made their home in the Egyptian desert, living in solitude and asceticism, believing they could achieve a higher spiritual and moral state by practicing self-denial, self-mortification, and sexual abstinence. Granted, they were on the far end of the spectrum; but they were still on the spectrum.

These Desert Fathers taught a division between a pure spirit and a sensual body. This belief caused them some theological difficulty when they began to ponder the story of Christ's incarnation. Why did God take on flesh if the flesh was wicked? "What is the purpose of this mixture of body and soul?" asked the Desert Father John Climacus. It wasn't a rhetorical question. He genuinely didn't have the philosophical framework to answer the question.

Father Climacus pondered another, related question: Those monks who struggled with sensuality tended to be more in touch with other people and simply more enjoyable than those "harsh dry" monks for whom chastity came more easily and naturally. Another paradox that Father Climacus seemed reluctant to consider in detail was how the same perceptiveness that enables a lover to sense the deepest movements of the soul in the body of his beloved, also enables him to have a perceptive spiritual vision of other people.[3] This obvious interconnection of body and soul brought to question the three centuries of "spiritual wisdom" he had inherited in the Egyptian desert.

Father Climacus's uncomfortable observations point to a truth that he was ill-equipped to grasp: Our sexual longings aren't simply an unfortunate fact of life in this body. If we let them, they point us toward a fuller understanding of what it means to love God with our whole selves—and how to love our neighbors as ourselves. Far from debasing us, our sexuality can exalt us to a place that is well beyond our bodies.

Pagan religions throughout the centuries and throughout the world have often acknowledged this truth that the Desert Fathers and other Christian teachers have sought to suppress. From the fertility rites of the Ancient Near East to the lusty gods of the Greek and Roman tradition, "pagan" religion has often been characterized by the recognition that there is something transcendent about our sexuality. The body, in these traditions, was viewed as sacred and stirring with new life. The ever-turning circles of the seasons celebrated birth, intercourse, and death. Sexual love and desire were viewed as divine; indeed, the ability to produce offspring was a vitally important blessing in a world where the average age rarely exceeded forty.

Now I'm not holding up pagan fertility rites—with their temple prostitution, ritual rape, and bestiality—as examples of healthy sexual expression. I merely observe that throughout human history, people have acknowledged a connection between sexual expression and spiritual expression. And if we Christians are going to break that connection, we'd better have good biblical reasons for doing so.

I contend that the radical disconnect between sex and faith didn't come from the Bible. So where did it come from? Ironically, it came from the pagans. Gnostics, in their various forms, led many Christians astray with the notion that we human beings are spirits who have been trapped in a material world. The term "Gnostic" was applied to various early Christian sects that claimed direct personal knowledge beyond the Gospel or the Church hierarchy.[4] The Gnostic sect known as the Manicheans, with their sharply dualistic vision of the good soul and the evil body, had a pernicious influence. As a matter of fact, they counted among their numbers the young Augustine—later Saint Augustine— before he became a Christian.

On the other hand, the Greek philosophy of stoicism was another important source of the anti-body rhetoric of early Christianity. The Stoics taught that the body is a tomb. They believed passion, sexual love, and emotions were false and that a person who had attained moral and intellectual perfection would not experience them.

The teachings of Gnostics and Stoics alike ignored the possibility that sexual love and desire were gifts from an unseen and untouchable God that provide an extraordinary opportunity to know and sense Him more intimately. As Christianity continued to flourish, these teachings began to permeate culture and emphasized the *danger* of sexual expression rather than its *divine* nature. Permanent celibacy became the ideal as Christianity spread.

In the desert, Father Climacus expressed an idealistic hope that human beings could somehow transcend the contradiction of soul and body. His hope was that he would someday look upon those who were formerly objects of sexual desire and see, not a body that would lead him into temptation, but the inner beauty of the created form. He wrote, "There was a man who, having looked upon a body of great beauty, at once gave praise to its Creator, and after one look was stirred to love God and weep copiously."[5] In other words, he hoped one day to be so holy that the sinful exterior body would become transparent to his eye, and the inner beauty and grace of the soul would point him to God.

Roman Christian mosaic art illustrates this religious ideal by rendering Christ and His disciples with bodies of celestial grace and symmetry that shimmer as if in a surreal fantasy. The artists depict transparent physical bodies foreshadowing the hope of a future transformation unencumbered by fleshly lusts.

But what if our sexual desires are simply a fact of living in these bodies of ours? Do we have to give up on knowing God until those desires go away? For those of us who innately feel (much like the pagans of old) that sexual desire and expression comprise a natural and joyful way of life and worship, the idea of renunciation seems confusing and empty.

The Lie of Control

Why, through the centuries, has the Church worked so hard to control sexuality? Perhaps because sexuality is so wild and free. Our sexuality represents a kind of freedom that is hard (not impossible—hard) for organized religion to deal with. God has given each of His children the difficult gift of free will. The church, like a jealous mother, feels threatened and demands a co-dependent relationship with *her* children.

What makes the church jealous of our sexuality? Could it be that she fears what freedom can do to her children and consequently instills a co-dependent fear in us in order to *protect* us from ourselves? Nurturing this dysfunctional connection requires rigid control and excessive rules and so the wilder aspects of Christianity, such as sex and sexuality, are deemed taboo in the name of God's "love." This seems rather ironic in light of Jesus Christ's teaching in John 8:32: "We shall know the truth, and the truth shall make us *free.*" Instead of setting her children free, the institutional church by its very nature tends to nurture a co-dependent relationship.

The church believes that freedom gives each of us the power to create and also to destroy. She knows a sex drive that makes love and babies can also lead to divorce and murder. Likewise, the freedom given an artist to paint a nude body has the power to glorify the wonder of creation, but it also has the power to titillate and degrade.

The church also realizes that this extraordinary freedom, when in the hands of mere mortals, provides each of us the opportunity for an intimate connection to the very One who brought galaxies into existence. She knows this cosmic power also created us as sexual beings and she feels that it only stands to reason, the more freedom we are given, the more potential we have to abuse it.

The challenge for the mother church today lies in relinquishing control and exhibiting mercy and grace instead of shame and judgment. When we walk through the struggles of real life (and more of us have than not) functional and unconditional love promises that we walk not *through* judgment but *to* freedom.

The unconditional love of God leads to a life of freedom and transforms each day into a potentially wild adventure. The dysfunction of the church causes her to want to "fix" her children and act as the authority for our lives. This begs an important question: "Is the Church or the Creator the ultimate authority in our lives?"

A biblical understanding informs us that our ultimate authority must always be the Creator—not the Church or religion. Dysfunction comes when we intertwine the church and God and view them as one. We often forget that both church and religion consist of wayward leaders and broken people just like us. Our Creator alone earned the right to act as our ultimate authority and thus is worthy to receive the reciprocal gifts of intimacy and wild abandonment. He desires both our soul *and* body more than our religious minds can comprehend.

Jesus teaches that His Heavenly Father does not love us in a co-dependent way. Rather, He knows that no matter how much we struggle with Him, in our desperate and wayward searching, if we genuinely seek Truth, we will ultimately fall safely back into His arms.

On the Incarnation

The Bible teaches that God came to earth as man to redeem and yes, romance us in all that we are. God is the great Lover, pursuing us in a human body. If He had needed only to redeem our soul and spirit, He could have conceivably done so from heaven. However, He also desired to redeem our body and sexuality, and that required an extraordinary union of God and man, in the person of Jesus Christ. That union is what we call the Incarnation.

"As Christians, we worship a God who at a specific time in history became a man, a spiritual Creator who became a physical creature," wrote Louis Markos. "The greatest miracle of our faith, I would argue, is not the Resurrection but the Incarnation. Christ (the Word made flesh) is the middle ground where God and man, spiritual and physical, meet and join hands across a divide."[6] A clear and true understanding of the greatest miracle—that of Incarnation—must be at the foundation of all that we are.

The Son of God chose to walk on earth in human flesh to redeem our bodies and experience our every desire. Because of that, He knows our limitations. God understands that we tend to search for love in all the wrong places. And because we look mostly in sensual areas, "God became Himself an object for the senses and took to Himself a body and moved as Man among men, in effect 'meeting our senses'...and so by His own power He restored the whole nature of man."[7]

There are many ways to look at the human body. We can admire it as the noblest of God's creations, despise it as the prison of the soul, worship it as the temple of love, fear it as the source of temptation, or study it as a scientific object.[8]

Sometimes, the body longs for God in the most paradoxical of ways. Could it be, as one writer puts it, that every knock at the door of a brothel is actually a knock at the heart of God?

We who have practiced religion squirm at questions such as these. We know the eternal God knew yearning and desire long before we did. The Bible teaches that He created us in His image and desires to be our consummate Lover.

Religious lies lead us to believe that if we ask God to join us in our most intimate moments, all our fantasies, fun and games will be over. But on the contrary, my friend, dare to read on and we will together seek to understand how true intimacy with the Almighty can possibly make the greatest sexual experience of your life seem tame in comparison.

part II. lies

2.

the lie about nudity

"Man is the sole animal whose nudity offends his own companions, and the only one who, in his natural actions, withdraws and hides himself from his own kind."
Montaigne

Michelangelo's overwhelming incarnation of man stands tall in Florence, Italy. Recognized universally as one of humanity's greatest works of art, *David* seems primed for both a sensual and spiritual struggle. In *David*, mankind was reimagined as transcendent and full of power. Passionately believing sculpture to be the only artistic expression that mimics divine creation, Michelangelo rendered *David* from a single block of gleaming Carrara marble.

After a lifetime of anticipation and with a pounding heart, I found myself walking down a narrow, white marble hallway lined with chiseled busts. The sea of gawking humanity was gathered in a gallery created especially for the towering masterpiece. I drew close and looked up in wonder as luminous light from a glass dome bathed *David* in a heavenly glow. As I moved breathlessly around the statue, I realized at every angle, though sculpted in marble, life pulsed within. At that moment, it seemed to me as though the world may have been created just to house this magnificent monument.

Because of its incredible size, the statue has been referred to as *Il Gigante* or The Giant, standing almost 17 feet tall. As my wife stood in front of *David*, I could not help but notice her rapturous, yet slightly uncomfortable gaze at his *Il Gigante*—his very large, uncircumcised genitalia, complete with pubic hair.

David is completely and beautifully nude. Muscles ripple across his torso and his body exudes taut sensuality. Michelangelo took great care in defining, even celebrating, every curve and every line of the human form. So when I later discovered that an exact replica of *David* at the Victoria and Albert Museum in England had a detachable plaster fig leaf for most of the 19th Century, I was a little surprised.

Male nudity was a contentious issue in the Victorian

era. A letter sent to the Museum in 1903 by a Mr. Dobson complained about the statue: "One can hardly designate these figures as 'art'! If it is, it is a very objectionable form of art."[1]

But before we judge our predecessors too harshly, here is a perfect example of how modernity has reacted to nudity in today's culture. The website www.statues.com actually offers the option of a covered *David*. The ad copy reads "Michelangelo would be offended! But for those individuals or educational organizations who would rather display him with covered private parts...this is the only place to find Michelangelo's *David* sculpture, covered up!" Let's just admit it. We don't quite know what to do with *David*.

Nudity and Art

In his travel guide to Italy, Rick Steves says that while the formal subject of the statue is biblical—*David* slaying the giant—in actuality, it's a classical nude, a celebration of the human body. In only a generation's time before *David* was created, a celebrated nude sculpture or painting would have been shocking. Before the Renaissance, this type of art was legitimate only if it "glorified God." Most of its kind sat clothed deep in the cavities of churches and were related to a Bible story.

With the Renaissance (the term literally means rebirth), man—unashamed and undaunted—stepped out from the shroud of religious institution. People finally began to realize the best way to glorify God was to recognize their talents and use them. The Church could no longer be allowed to control and keep the arts within its walls. And as if to illustrate this fact, the finished *David* was placed in the glorious open air of the public plaza of Florence, the spacious Piazza della Signoria. There he stood proudly for three hundred years until the statue was reluctantly moved inside the walls of the gallery due to damage from weather and pollution.

Only a short walk from the glory of *David* stands the extraordinary Uffizi Gallery of Art where the vast array of stunning rooms and artistic masterpieces provides a rare chronological and visual glimpse through history. As I explored the many hallways and galleries, I first saw man depicted without expression and dimension in early frescoes and altarpieces of orthodoxy. The melancholy experience of viewing one-dimensional religious art and expressionless faces was not lost on me and I pondered what kind of strict and unforgiving religion these masters subscribed to.

But as I walked in wonder through the door of the Botticelli room, I felt as if I had crossed a sensual and spiritual threshold from cold darkness and despair to warm sunlight and delight. In front of me stood a voluptuous woman, blown by the winds of spiritual passion. It was Sandro Botticelli's painting, *The Birth of Venus*, and is considered among the most treasured masterpieces of the Renaissance.

Botticelli celebrated mankind by depicting the human body with vibrant colors, vivid light, and transparent adornments. His paintings seem to shimmer with celestial harmony and beauty.

At this time in history, when almost all art was Christian themed, the portrayal of nudes in the west had decreased drastically. Nude women were rare and only depicted sinful lust. "Virtually the only permissible nudity for centuries was in religious art, with painted and sculpted depictions of Adam and Eve (though they were often discreetly draped) and in some Last Judgment scenes. Nudity was used in such art as a signifier of shame...a far cry from the open and frequent display of perfect nude bodies in ancient Greece for the delight of viewers," says Professor Ellen Graves in a *Brief History of the Nude in Art*.

Most paintings of women during the Middle Ages symbolized the Virgin Mary, showing her in a demure appearance and covered head. Yet, the nude *Venus* is a beautiful and chaste goddess, and symbol of the coming spring. She is everything opposite of the sinful lust attributed

c. 1485, *tempera on canvas*
Galleria degli Uffizi, Florence

to the naked female body.

So why did these deeply religious artistic masters, Michelangelo and Botticelli, create their most beautiful works as sensuous nudes? It seems that both somehow innately understood that by portraying spirituality and sensuality, they were simply rendering mankind as God had originally intended.

Both *David* and *The Birth of Venus* serve as reminders that our sense of beauty provides the means to reunite with something completely beyond ourselves. Both provide portrayals of nudity and sacramental beauty that have withstood the ages and fires of religious lies. We have only just begun to uncover the truth they have to offer concerning our own sexuality.

Nudity and the Bible

The Hebrew Bible says that God created man and was pleased with his naked beauty. The Bible describes both man and woman as unclothed and feeling no shame. And although God created them nude, subsequently it was Adam and Eve who covered themselves and hid in shame—not from each other—but from God.

We know that Adam and Eve were ashamed but is it possible that they did not want God to look upon their nakedness because they realized their intimacy with God was irretrievably forfeited? What if they were ashamed of what they had lost (an intimate connection) rather than ashamed of their nakedness?

Every child who attends Sunday school or church is taught this story, and from a young age, we learn that nudity is bad. But Scripture does not seem to place explicit restrictions on nudity. In fact, King David danced partially nude as he publicly celebrated the news of the Ark of the Covenant's return. Even the prophets often spoke of nakedness as a symbol of poverty—being stripped of everything, including clothes. In both instances, the nakedness isn't associated with sexuality or sensuality. But that's not to say that God doesn't approve of either sensuality or sexuality.

In fact, God openly celebrates the nude body and the beauty of sex through imagery in the Song of Songs. Although many religious theologians attempt to explain away the sexual eroticism of this poetry by saying it only represents a conversation between Christ and His church expressing their esteem for each other, a careful reading of the Song of Songs reveals a multi-layered and multi-sensual masterpiece.

Professor Bruce Bezaire of O'More College of Design says that, "It is first and literally an erotic poem and secondly and more profoundly a picture—in terms we can understand—of the intimacy we as the bride of Christ can anticipate in a perfected relationship with our bridegroom in the future consummation." In this context, consummation carries a layered nuance of bringing to a state of completion and also the union of a marriage.

In the Song of Songs, the best of all songs, the bronzed beauty that is Solomon's lover celebrates all, and I mean *all* of his body, from his red-blooded radiance, his raven black curls, his dove-like eyes soft and bright, his aromatic beard, and his torso hard and smooth as ivory. She calls him a rugged mountain of a man, tall like a cedar, strong and deep-rooted.

The last chapters rise to a climax of antiphonal songs and choruses in which the man and woman try to out do each other with vivid and erotic descriptions of their respective bodies. Finally, they both verbally paint her body in a ravishing description of ecstasy:

> Man: "My lover and friend, you're a secret garden,
> a private and pure fountain."

> Woman: Oh, let my lover enter his garden!
> Yes, let him eat the fine, ripe fruits."

> Man: "I went to the garden, dear friend, best lover!
> Breathed the sweet fragrance.
> I ate the fruit and honey,
> I drank the nectar and wine."

> Woman: "My lover is already on his way to the garden,
> To browse among the flowers, touching the colors and
> forms.
> I am my lover's and my lover is mine.
> He caresses the sweet-smelling flowers."[2]

A more poetic and affirmative description of nude beauty and sexual enjoyment would be hard to find. Reading the allusive and indirect language of the Song of Songs reveals many erotic delights. And yet, it provides much more. The book tells in extraordinary prose a story of mutual love and admiration encompassing both the sensual and spiritual mysteries of two gloriously nude lovers.

It seems ironic there are so many religious leaders who proclaim that every single word in the Bible is true, yet these same people have somehow overlooked verses such as these and teach that sexuality and nudity are less than holy. It's not like this is some kind of ancient forbidden pornographic text. This is the Bible.

Nudity and Nakedness

The sensual and spiritual aspects of the nude human body and of sexual love have inspired artists throughout history. Even today, we each have a hunger to behold the human body in its nakedness. "This hunger manifests a God-given yearning for beauty, a God-given desire for the 'great mystery' revealed by the body. Each person must decide whether he remains only a superficial 'consumer' of the pornography that incessantly bombards us, or commits to the effort of drawing near to the glorious truth of the human body in all its masculinity and femininity."[3]

The Bible says we were created in the likeness of God. Therefore, the external human body, in its original created beauty, is rich in meaning and provides a glimpse of the internal soul. But as we seek to remove restraints from the body that centuries of religion have placed upon it, the enormity of this task begins to dawn. There are no simple conclusions. We can debate the pros and cons of religious history, but we will never have agreement on the issue of nudity.

Many religious people will say, "The naked body will always arouse lust in man." For the person controlled by lust, that may very well be true. But not all people are controlled by lust and not all people view nudity in the same way. John Berger says it this way, "Nakedness reveals itself. Nudity is placed on display. The nude is condemned to never being naked. Nudity is a form of dress." To me, as an artist, this means that nudity reveals the theology of the body, while nakedness ignores it.

If we were to take the words of the Hebrew Bible to

heart, we would see that we have been set *free* from the control of sin, and that includes the sin of lust. We have been given the gift of love and purity. When we live out this life by daily accepting the gift of redemption, we are unconditionally set free from prudishness and suspicion, and lust will not control our being.

This means we cannot simply equate nudity with immodesty and lust. If we think "a lustful look" is the only way a person can look at the human body, then we subscribe to what John Paul II calls the "interpretation of suspicion." Sadly, those who live a life of suspicion remain so imprisoned by their own lusts that they try to exert that same bondage on everyone else. They can't think of the body and sex other than through the prism of lust.

If we focus on living a life of control (and suspicion) instead of living a life of freedom (and acceptance) we grow cynical and self-serving. When I say a life of freedom, I am talking about freedom within the bounds of truth. This kind of suspicion essentially cuts us off from the enjoyment of the wonder and beauty of God's love and creation. So do we choose to be controlled by lust or freed by Christ?

The human body is indeed a symbol of God's mystery. The human body itself becomes in some sense a sacrament, that is, a sign that makes visible the invisible mystery of God. Jesus Christ in the Sermon on the Mount said, "Blessed are the pure in heart, for they shall *see* God" (Matt. 5:8). God wants to reveal Himself to us. He wants to make His "feast of beauty" visible to us so that we can "see" Him.

And what better way to see God than in the ultimate creation? "God created man in his own image, in the image of God he created them, male and female. And God blessed them...and said that it was good" (Genesis 1:27-28). Purity of heart lets us look at the human body (ours and our neighbors) and see divine beauty—the invisible God made visible. As Pope John Paul II states, "Those who revel in God's freedom view nakedness and nudity as a manifestation of divine beauty—a revelation of God's plan of love."[4]

3.

the lie about beauty

"Beauty...is the shadow of God on the universe."
Gabriela Mistral

One of the desirable elements of art is beauty and when an artist combines beauty with the provocative sensuality of the nude body, confusion occurs in some viewers regarding the issue of vulgarity. This brings up the basic aspect of beauty in art, and its uneasy relationship with religion.

Girolamo Savonarola was an Italian Dominican priest and leader of Florence, Italy, from 1494 until his execution in 1498. He utilized a popular bully pulpit to rail against makeup, jewelry, hairpieces, and what he described as "lewd" paintings. While the great artist Botticelli celebrated life and beauty in paintings such as the *Birth of Venus*, the religious leader Savonarola carried out his infamous "Bonfire of the Vanities" at the Piazza Della Signoria, in Florence, Italy, determined to destroy the trappings of luxury and immoral excesses.

Botticelli came under the influence of this Dominican zealot and reputedly burned many of his own "pagan" works. As I viewed the Botticelli paintings exhibited chronologically at the Uffizi Gallery, I noted an unmistakable change taking place. His work becomes religious in nature and much more medieval in its look. Some historians say he eventually quit painting altogether. Many great artists of that time were affected by these religious lies. "Nearly sixty years later, Michelangelo told a friend that he could still hear the terrible voice of Savonarola resounding in his ears."[1]

Somehow, the vibrant and sensual *Birth of Venus* was spared the flames of Savonarola's hypocrisy, most likely due to Botticelli's friendship with the great patron of the arts, Lorenzo de Medici. The masterpiece remained safe from the holocaust of religious fervor in a Medici villa outside Florence.

In a twist of fate, the same Piazza Della Signoria where the Bonfire of the Vanities took place and countless works of priceless art were lost in flames, witnessed the execution by fire of Father Savonarola. He was hanged in chains from a single cross and an enormous fire was lit beneath him. The Friar was executed in the same manner that he had condemned other "criminals" and works of art during his reign in Florence. The executioner lit the flame exclaiming, "The one who wanted to burn me is now himself put to the flames."[2] Savonarola's ashes were carefully stirred and thrown into the river Arno so that his fanatical followers could not venerate the slightest piece. Ironically, six years later, the very same Piazza della Signoria that witnessed the Bonfire of the Vanities and Savonarola's subsequent execution, became a marble cathedral for the "lewd" statue of *David*.

This lifeless orthodoxy, as Savonarola personified, has permeated society in the name of religion. And it was exactly what Jesus spoke vehemently against in Matthew 23:13 when He rebuked the religious leaders of His time— the Pharisees—calling them "hypocrites, fools, and liars" who "shut the door to the kingdom of heaven in people's faces. Not going in themselves, and not allowing those who are trying to enter to go in."

Throughout history, religious zealots such as these have spent their lifetimes attempting to shield the eyes of others from the natural beauty of creation. Ashamed of the harmony and beauty they have allowed to wither in themselves, their warped ideology causes them to destroy anything in their path that awakens a hunger for the communion with God they have somehow lost or intentionally suffocated.

Although it may seem noble to "save" morality by giving it a more "sacred" basis, the result is division between mankind and religion, between facts and values, and between history and myth. One needs only to peruse history for many chilling examples.

Early Christianity had the aforementioned Pharisees who created thousands of rules and regulations even as Jesus was teaching that truth equals freedom. The Middle Ages saw priceless art destroyed in religious "holy" wars called the Crusades. History records the controlling censorship of myriad religious leaders.

This division is not limited to the past. Modern times brought the omission of art in churches by American fundamentalist religious leaders and the banning of photography and suppression of artists by radical Muslim sects. These are only a few of the many manifestations of historical "Savonarolas."

Nudity and Beauty

Nudity has the power to incite emotions such as surprise, uneasiness, and intimacy. Each of us has positive and negative life experiences that cause us to react when confronted with artistic portrayals of the body *au naturel*. Unfortunately, for a large percentage, the reaction is more uncomfortable and is the result of a flawed introduction to sexuality at an early age.

In *Portrait of an Artist as a Young Man,* James Joyce writes that his alter ego, Stephen, while walking an isolated beach, suddenly spies a beautiful young girl looking out to sea. As he gazes upon her unclothed body, her slender legs, her bare thighs, her soft breasts and her fair hair, she feels his presence and "the worship of his eyes," and turns to him without "shame or wantonness."

Their eyes lock for what must have seemed eternity, but then again, for what surely must have seemed only a moment. There were no words exchanged. He describes that moment later as "a holy silence of ecstasy," saying that "her eyes had called him and his soul had leaped at the call."[3]

This story provides a perfect example of the paradox of naked beauty. Could a moment such as this be what Desert Father Climacus idealized as he longed for the day when nudity would be sensed with unaccustomed intensity, but without temptation? Is this ideal of "holy longing" even possible? To explore this question further, we need to journey back in time to a philosopher, theologian, musician and Roman Catholic priest.

Thomas Aquinas (1225–1274) lived at a critical time in history when the arrival of translated versions of Aristotle's body of work reopened the question of the relation between faith and reason. Aquinas had extraordinary qualifications as a priest but was also a philosopher *and* theologian *and* musician. Umberto Eco writes in *The Aesthetics of Thomas Aquinas*, "when Aquinas wrote about beauty and artistic form he was not dealing with mere abstractions, cut off from experience. He was referring, implicitly, to a world which he knew well."[4]

Aquinas writes in his magnificent work *Summa Theologica* that three things are needed for beauty: harmony, wholeness and radiance.

- *Harmony* (Aquinas calls it *proportio*) refers to the arrangement of the parts of a work and the sum of the relationships between them. Harmonic notes in music are separate, yet they move together while complementing one another.

- *Wholeness* (Aquinas calls it *integritas*) exists in a work that lacks nothing essential to its full being. It provides a full understanding and portrayal; something that is complete in all its parts.

• *Radiance* (Aquinas calls it *claritas*) speaks of that which makes a thing clearly seen for what it is. It is that feeling that goes with you as you depart. You feel as if you leave a better person having been in the presence of true beauty.

These elements of beauty may help resolve a personal dilemma when we next face a naked beauty in a gallery, on a beach, or on a computer screen. They provide guidelines for the artist or viewer to understand whether the nudity they encounter is beautiful or pornographic. A nude portrayed or viewed utilizing these premises embodies the glory of the human body rather than an objectification of it.

The Difference Between Beauty and Pornography

When we take off our clothes in lovemaking, it represents a revealing of sexual and spiritual secrets between lovers. Therefore the truthful artist, in depicting exposed flesh and the intense passion of the sex act, speaks in a way that portrays both a spiritual and sensual communion. In many works that overemphasize titillating aspects, the artist doesn't show too much, but on the contrary, *he shows too little.*

For example, in the sculpture, *The Rape of the Sabine Women*, (rape in this context signifies kidnapping—not forced sex) three beautifully nude and provocative figures engage in an intensely passionate struggle. While hopelessly intertwined, the two males and one female arouse many responses. The method in which the artist, Giambologna, poses the statue, provides multiple viewpoints of the unfolding drama. These aspects provide opportunity for the thoughtful viewer to fully identify with the mystery and inner emotions of the subjects while also sensing the erotic nature of the story.

When judged against the Aquinas three aspects of beauty, *The Rape of the Sabine Women* fully passes the test. The viewer can understand the *wholeness* and completeness

of the story. One can understand its *harmony* and feel the rhythm, conflict and interaction of the characters with each other. The sculptures' *radiance* provides an understanding of what the artist might have felt creating the piece, a surreal pleasure upon viewing, and an afterglow that only slowly fades.

When these elements of beauty mysteriously connect the artist with the viewer, there is a sense of satisfaction and revelation. The wholeness, harmony, and radiance provide the viewer, as Luigi Galvani calls it, "an enchantment of the heart." But this is vastly different from the act of viewing pornography.

When subjected to the question of *harmony*, the actors in a pornographic film are portrayed as partial rather than whole beings. In fact, once a perception of completeness enters the story (for example, realizing the character is someone's son or daughter who possibly has been abused and coerced) it diminishes the pornography's ability to titillate.

The pornographer causes the viewer to subjectively respond to the person or act portrayed only as a means of personal gratification. Creators of pornography sell a perception that sexual fulfillment represents the only value of a person and that meaning exists only in fleshly aspects. There is no opportunity to respond to either the *wholeness* or *harmony* of that person or to the *mysteries* and *radiance* of the sexual act. As far as the question of radiance, there remains no "all is right in the world" feeling, or leaving a better person, or a sense of the lingering presence of true beauty.

Another test of art versus pornography is whether the subject's nudity makes him or her seem more or less human. Does it enable you to identify with the subject, or does it distance you from the subject, allowing you to view that figure as an object rather than as a complete person?

Within the context of love, a mutual giving and receiving takes place, leading to the orgasmic pleasure of sexual intimacy. Through intercourse, we share with our lover what is ours to give. This personal giving and receiving unites our souls so exclusively, that for another person to view or partake in the sharing of this erotic gift violates an exclusive communion. There remains no room for a *ménage a trois.*

Unfortunately, there are many creators in the entertainment industry who market their media by presenting shallow and explicit sexual activities that leave the consumer empty and devoid of *radiance.* These pornographers trivialize and exploit the naked body and sex act as merely selfish entertainment and choose to ignore the potential for sensual and spiritual intimacy and healthy love.

The question is, can art adequately portray the truth concerning the mysterious union that is uniquely expressed between intimate lovers without being pornographic? Some say yes. Bruce Bezaire, Professor of Art, states, "A fundamental aspect of art is allusion or indirectness. Does the image represent or simply present?" When judging the presented or represented image against Aquinas' elements of wholeness, harmony and radiance, the answer becomes clear. Even Pope John Paul II in his epic *Theology of the Body* states, "A masterful artist can lead us through the naked body to the whole personal mystery of man (and woman) and allow us to comprehend the sexual union of the body in purity of heart." He goes on to say that an artist's work manifests "his inner world of values."[5]

Christopher West, the man who has rendered Pope John Paul's epic *Theology of the Body* understandable to the common man relates the story about a woman modeling for art students. Having disrobed before the students, she suddenly covered herself when she noticed the shade had not been drawn on the window. When the teacher apologized and drew the shade, she again disrobed. This vividly demonstrates that her nudity before the students was not "shameless" but a form of "nakedness without shame." She trusted the students to respect her "gift of nudity" and to respond to it in an equally personal way. However, shame immediately manifested itself (and rightly so) when she realized that her nakedness was being potentially exposed to an unknown (and, therefore, untrusted) audience.

Both with the sculpture of *David* and the painting of *Venus*, the sexual values of the nude figures harmonize with spiritual values to portray wholeness, harmony, and radiance while not drawing unbalanced attention to the interior or the exterior. When these and other creations of art honestly render the nude body, one is not compelled by their subject matter toward an exclusively shallow or lustful response. On the contrary, forthright art inspires one to reflect upon the being of the person, whether clothed or unclothed.

Religious lies cause many to question the integrity of any model who poses nude or any artist who portrays the nude body. Likewise, the nude paintings by Michelangelo that grace the extraordinary ceiling of the Sistine Chapel were judged obscene by religious leaders and were later painted over with clumsily rendered coverings. Pope John Paul II strongly asserts, "This only demonstrated a sense of the viewers impurity; that is, their own inability to see the body as a theology, a revelation of the mystery of God. The naked body is not obscene. What is obscene is that which specifically attempts to stir lust."[6] If such a pious man as the Pope can see this truth, why is it that the majority of religious teachers and subscribers can't?

4.

the lie about self-pleasure

"Simple pleasures are always the last refuge of the complex."
Oscar Wilde

I'm not blind and neither are you. But the terrifying imagery taught by religion concerning masturbation has wreaked havoc on the normal healthy sexual function of many young adolescents and adults alike. The guilt associated with this form of self-pleasure is all the more unfortunate in light of the fact that the entire perspective on masturbation is based upon a completely unbiblical interpretation of the story of Onan.

As the story goes, while refusing to ejaculate inside his brother's wife, as directed by God, Onan intentionally spilled his semen on the ground to prevent her getting pregnant by him (Gen. 38:9). His error was not in masturbating, but that he refused to follow God's directive to perpetuate the name and lineage of his deceased brother. This story has been told to Christians everywhere as the basis for proving the evils of masturbation.

The narrative of Genesis 38 describes required behavior within Israelite families, and its purpose was filled with wisdom and probably originated in the pagan culture of Egypt or Babylon. Its threefold design was to first, reproduce the name of a man who died without an heir, second, provide legal clarity, and third, ensure that his widow had a care-giver. However, for some unknown reason, Onan did not want to ejaculate inside his sister-in-law Tamar. Perhaps he already had too many children and his brother had left no inheritance. Whatever the reason, it is very apparent that God killed him for coitus interruptus (which means he deliberately interrupted sex by withdrawing his penis from her vagina prior to ejaculation), and disobedience—not masturbation. By misconstruing the true meaning, religious leaders use this passage as a proof text to teach the evils of masturbation.

Others also condemn self-pleasure. A representative of the Mormon Church states in an official publication called "To Young Men Only": "There is; however, something you should not do. Sometimes a young man does not understand. Perhaps he is encouraged by unwise or unworthy companions to tamper with that "factory." He might fondle himself and open that release valve. This you shouldn't do, for if you do that, the little factory will speed up. You will then be tempted again and again to release it. You can quickly be subjected to a habit, one that is not worthy, one that will leave you feeling depressed and feeling guilty. Resist that temptation. Do not be guilty of tampering or playing with this sacred power of creation. Keep it in reserve for the time when it can be righteously employed."[1]

One possible reason for the forbidding of self-pleasure may derive from the early church doctrines on birth control and procreation. Within the context of marriage, masturbation was viewed as a form of preventing conception. So they reasoned that any sexual act used for anything other than reproduction is a sin against God's will and God's design for humans. Although much can be said about this theologically, philosophically, and morally, that discussion is beyond the scope of this book. Let's instead explore self-pleasure and also discuss aspects of personal and mutual pleasuring.

Pleasure

A definition of masturbation reads: "the act of achieving sexual release by oneself through stimulating the erogenous zones of the body."[2] The word itself raises all sorts of misunderstanding, guilt, and taboos. Dr. Douglas Roseau, a licensed Psychologist and Marriage and Family Therapist specializing in sex therapy, states: "Myths existed even in medical textbooks into the 1930s about masturbation causing psychoses, 'lunacy,' blindness, and many other mental and physical problems. Supposedly, people could identify such self-abusers by the way they walked and their stunted physical development."[3]

To further illustrate how false religious teaching permeates the fabric of our society, one only need go to the reference shelves of our libraries. Unbelievably, _Webster's Revised Unabridged Dictionary_ defines masturbation as: _Onanism; self-pollution._[4]

The truth is that scripture does not address the subject of masturbation. It does, however, talk a lot about the beauty of pleasure. As we've learned in earlier chapters, for some reason, religion has sacrificed pleasure at the cross of self-denial. We somehow feel as western Christians, that we don't deserve pleasure. Alexander Schmemann convincingly says, "The religious perspective of a dichotomy of the body and soul, spiritual and material, sacred and profane, is nowhere to be found in Scripture." He goes on to say that, "The world as man's food is not something exclusively 'material' and thus opposed to the 'spiritual.' All that exists is God's gift to man, and it all exists to make God known to man, and is given as communion with God. God blesses everything He creates (including pleasure) and in biblical language, this means that He makes all creation the sign and means of His presence and wisdom, love and revelation: 'O taste and see that the Lord is good.'"[5]

The Bible begins with man as a sexual being and with God pronouncing it good. God created us with the ability to experience and enjoy pleasure. It would be a cruel joke indeed if God gave us genitals and hands, and then commanded that we never touch. However, we would be remiss to overlook the dangers of "an ever-increasing craving of an ever-diminishing pleasure."[6] As one counselor says, "The question is not *if* you masturbate, but *how often*?" Just as with any other human behavior, if an unhealthy addiction develops that consumes your daily life, it may be time to seek a licensed sex therapist.

Unhealthy Self-Pleasure

There are four issues that will help us evaluate unhealthy masturbation practices from a spiritual perspective. First, the practice of masturbation is often associated with sexual fantasy, voyeurism, and pornography. When this practice becomes "ever-increasing," these associations can possibly lead to mental pollution, and because of "an ever-diminishing" pleasure, it can lead to overt acts of aggression in order to experience the same level of self-satisfaction.

Second, masturbation runs the risk of becoming a compulsive behavior pattern. "In this way it can lead to deep problems of guilt or self-abasement."[7] This compulsive behavior (much the same as eating disorders or alcoholism) may be a red flag, which indicates a deeper problem that requires professional help.

Third, addictive behavior can lead to dysfunction within a sexual relationship, especially if it results in a selfish disregard of the other's sexual needs. While some erotics and sexual devices are acceptable, a problem should be recognized if methods such as pornography and other artificial means are the only way to achieve arousal and orgasm.

Finally, individual masturbation is ultimately an "ever-diminishing" pleasure and should not be viewed as the exclusive expression of mature human sexuality.

Healthy Self-Pleasure

Despite these cautions, self-pleasure does offer positive benefits. There is a reason God gave us hands and genitals with a complementary physical proximity. So let's examine a healthy perspective of each of the four unhealthy practices as previously discussed.

First, masturbation can be practiced without unhealthy sexual fantasy, voyeurism, or pornography. For instance, marriage and family therapist Betty Tyndall advised her son-in-law, an Army Chaplain charged with assisting young adults in their spiritual needs before they are deployed overseas, to have the soldiers take photographs, lingerie, underwear or other sensual items to remind them of their lover as they masturbate. It seemed commonsense to Betty that masturbation employed in this way results in a far more spiritually mature outcome than imagining sex with other people or having sexual intercourse with a prostitute.

Another spiritually mature sexual practice that new technology affords for businessmen and women who are away extended periods of time to take along digital erotic photographs of their lover as a means for arousal during masturbation rather than pornography or an illicit tryst with another person. Obviously, there would need to be care taken to protect this material and keep it private.

Second, understand that when the goal of masturbation is an occasional release for pent-up sexual energy, it can provide a positive and healthy outcome. This becomes particularly important in the long-term absence of a mate. It also provides a compromise when one mate enjoys sex far more than the other. For instance, Dr. Rosenau tells of a wife who was too tired from her daily duties to have sex every night. But she didn't mind pleasuring her husband who desired sex each evening to an orgasm without her active participation. She would slip off her nightgown and gently hold his testicles while he stroked himself to a climax. This technique revolutionized their sex lives.[8]

Third, self or mutual pleasure through the act of masturbation can provide excitement and pleasure that is physically impossible for your mate to provide. "Almost two-thirds of women cannot achieve orgasm without direct stimulation of the clitoris."[9] For those women, self or mutual pleasure before and during intercourse can lead to an orgasm that cannot be attained otherwise. Self-pleasure for the entertainment and arousal of your mate during sexual intercourse may also result in unexpected benefits. Gifts such as more frequent and more intense orgasms for both partners as well as a higher frequency in sexual encounters may occur.

There are other reasons why masturbation might be necessary in a relationship. Many find themselves with a partner who cannot physically consummate the sexual act. Prostate cancer, limb paralysis, and other maladies may render libido impossible. In such cases, self-pleasure may be the only spiritually mature recourse. Ideally, the limited partner would participate as much as possible, but if mentally, emotionally or physically incapable (such as after prostate surgery) the remaining partner should feel free of guilt to enjoy personal self-pleasure within healthy dimensions.

And finally, God designed us so that sexual intimacy between two lovers in a mutual relationship results in "ever-increasing" pleasure. Learn to play together. Dr. Rosenau says, "Enjoying genital pleasuring that is slow and bonding without pressure and demands is critical to a truly intimate, nurturing and exciting sex life."[10]

Another exquisite invention of technology is a vibrator. This tool can be a very useful means of exploring and expanding sexual response. Although vibrators are most commonly associated with a woman's pleasure, they are equally effective for men. Couples can heighten their sexual enjoyment by utilizing a vibrator with each other to produce intense pleasure. For instance, if a man is physically tired or emotionally stressed, he or his mate may "enclose the penis within the fist and place the vibrator on the outside, so that the vibration goes through the hand and into the penis."[11] This will often produce an erection.

Guilt

For many of us with a religious background, guilt is passed down by our parents and other role models, and an unfortunate portrayal of God is ingrained into our psyche. The only verse that we remember (albeit out of context) is, "whom God loves, He chastens." Robert Burns' words are a perfect example:

> *For guilt, for guilt, my terrors are in arms:*
> *I tremble to approach an angry God,*
> *And justly smart beneath His sin-avenging rod.*[12]

Our picture of God could be likened to Heath Ledger's portrayal of the Joker in the film *The Dark Knight*, with a huge taser, ready to disable us at the slightest hint of impropriety. And our guilt-ridden beliefs about sexual pleasure can be likened to nectar licked from a razor's edge.

Let's face it. We don't really believe in grace. We have an Old Testament view of an angry God of judgment and control, rather than a Savior of mercy and freedom. The leaders who represent religion often enhance our distorted view of guilt. Handing down the dysfunction of the generations before them, they bequeath us an intolerant God.

As one growing up in a lifetime of religious guilt, it was not until recently that I realized my sexual desire was simply a hunger for a loving and seductive God. Through the direction of a gentle and grace-giving life coach during a very difficult season of life, I began to realize that, indeed, all the hunger of my life is ultimately for God. Despite religious leaders who have heaped judgment upon our longings, we must come to realize that spiritual (and sexual) freedom is a gift given by God that no one can take away.

Centuries of religious repression have failed to destroy the desires He has created in us. To experience pleasure is at its core, something more than masturbation or sexual intercourse. It is something more than eating and drinking. Schmemann says that, "we may not fully understand what that "something more" is, but nonetheless, we desire to celebrate it."[13]

In the movie *Chariots of Fire*, Eric Liddell famously says, "When I run, I feel God's pleasure." So, equipped with a proper understanding of the healthy and unhealthy aspects of self-pleasure, erasing all the religious guilt with the freedom of God's truth, and desiring a mutual relationship with God and others, the question may ultimately be, "When you masturbate, do you feel God's pleasure?" Because, literally, the answer is in your hands.

5.

the lie about sexual fantasy

"If your sexual fantasies were truly of interest to others, they would no longer be fantasies."
Fran Lebowitz

We are not taught much about the wilder aspects of sexuality. We fear wildness for much the same reason that people are afraid that fantasy is a "waste," and that erotic sex is somehow immoral, carnal, and not spiritual. But this sort of fear destroys the beauty and wonder of imaginative sexuality. It binds us where we should be free.

What if an understanding of our wild desires could provide us with a less restricted view of time and space and yes, even ourselves? What if God provided the gift of sexual imagination to provide a transcendent high far more satisfying than the most powerful drug? What if our fantasies have such an effect on us as lovers that it enlarges our limited sense of reality?

Sexual fantasy can provide a way to remember all the lovely things we have forgotten. In our acts of fantasy, our logical, prove-it-to-me minds relax and we begin to experience anew all that we felt as young lovers; the tingle in our stomach the first time we held hands, the sensual moistness of our first lingering kiss, and the ecstasy of making love for the first time with someone we really, truly, love.

Fantasy calls our imagination into vigorous play. But in spite of this obvious benefit, there are many who religiously refuse to exercise this gift. They avoid the demands of high-definition imagination or what Coleridge calls "the willing suspension of disbelief," choosing to live in a routine and selfish world of black and white.

We have been trained in a culture of instant gratification, and when more than a "quickie" sexual tryst is needed, we abandon the effort that selflessness requires and slink back to the safety of caring for children and meeting deadlines or the mindless passivity of television. In doing so, we trade the ultimate high of transcendent sexual relationship for the selfishness of what might as well be self-masturbation. This selfishness hurts both partners and can take a toll on the relationship because of a lack of intimacy and effort.

To better understand this wild and powerful gift, let's look first at a definition and short history of sexual fantasy, explore the fascinating results of our online survey, talk about healthy fantasy, and finally, delve into the extraordinary gift of imagination.

Sexual Fantasy

A sexual fantasy, or erotic fantasy, is a pattern of thoughts that creates or enhances sexual feelings. In short, it is almost any mental imagery that is sexually arousing or erotic. A fantasy can be a long, drawn-out story or a quick mental flash of sexual imagery. And its purpose can range from sexual motivations, such as sexual arousal and reaching orgasm, to simply passing time or helping a person fall asleep.

The moral acceptance and formal study of sexual fantasy in Western culture is relatively new. In the not-too-recent past, sexual fantasies were seen as evil or sinful, and they were commonly seen as horrid thoughts planted into the minds of people by "agents of the devil." The roots of Stoicism that remain in many of our religious teachings warn against emotion, imagination, and feelings, deeming anything other than logic and rational thought as lustful or weak.

Even when psychologists were willing to accept and study fantasies, they showed little understanding of the topic and even went so far as to diagnose sexual fantasies in females as a sign of hysteria. It's not hard to imagine then, that prior to the early twentieth century, many experts viewed sexual fantasy (particularly in females) as abnormal. Sigmund Freud suggested that those who experienced sexual fantasies were sexually deprived or frustrated or that they lacked adequate sexual stimulation and satisfaction.

We've definitely come a long way. Reading the previous paragraph seems almost laughable. Instead of viewing fantasy as abnormal, many of us today have an "anything goes" mentality. Perhaps, somewhere in between abnormal and "anything goes" rests a happy and mutually fulfilling playground for wild and sacred sexuality.

Fantasy in the Sex, Lies & Religion Survey

In preparation for this book, I administered an anonymous online survey at our website: www.sexliesandreligion.com. The results were fascinating to say the least. There were over 2,000 respondents of which over 95% indicated a religious affiliation and described themselves as spiritual.

- 34% of respondents said they fantasize during sex, but only 13% said they fantasize mutually in some way with their lover.

- When asked to describe their individual fantasies, almost 40% said they fantasize about making love with someone else other than their mate.

- 5% fantasize about some sort of bondage, spanking, or S&M. S&M is an abbreviation for two terms. Sadism is pleasure in the infliction of pain or humiliation upon another person, while masochism refers to gratification from receiving the same.[1]

• 5% fantasize about oral sex during sex.

• Various other fantasies included outdoor sex, risky sex, sex on a beach, romantic settings, multiple partners, being younger, reliving past sexual encounters, anal sex, different positions, gay or lesbian sex, sex with celebrities, movie scenes, role playing and more.

Of the 13% who said they enjoyed mutual fantasies with their lover, the results were as follows:

• 10% were about multiple partners, threesomes, and sex with strangers.

Others include role-playing, dressing up, domination, sex in a public place, outdoor sex, past sexual experiences, strangers who meet on a train, watching each other bring themselves to climax, and more.

The results were extremely revealing considering the amount of respondents who indicated they felt the survey was "not really anonymous." Some cited online privacy fears, some were afraid to be honest, and there was a conservative skew of the demographic information. One must also consider what the results would have been in a "safe" environment that was deemed by respondents as completely incognito.

Healthy Sexual Fantasy

A healthy fantasy life provides a wonderful opportunity to build a great sex life with our lover. The imagination is an erotic organ, in fact, the single most erotic organ in our body. To again quote respected Christian sex therapist Dr. Rosenau, "Your mind, with the ability to create and store information, is the central part of imagining and experiencing erotic pleasure. That is what sexual fantasy is all about: your mind, images that are paired with the sexual excitement, and your imagination to give them wings."[2]

One way to view healthy sexual fantasy for couples is a single phrase said by therapist Betty Tyndall, "Healthy sexual fantasy is anything that leads to oneness." Sounds familiar, doesn't it? We were created to leave our families to cleave to a mate and become "one flesh." Although Betty's prescription may sound restrictive, especially in light of the survey results previously mentioned, in reality, it leaves an enormous playground to enjoy.

Betty's mentor, Dr. Rosenau, has this to say about erotic fantasy, "Everyone has fantasies about other people, and they can be destructive to your commitment to building sexual intimacy. Fantasy is important but it should be centered on your mate and the fantastic sex life you are building together."[3]

Dr. Rosenau believes that sinful diluting of intimacy and acting out sexually are encouraged by continual, intentional fantasies about persons or situations outside of marriage. He also states the individual part of sexuality is hard to sort out. In fact, the personal fantasies that accompany masturbation or even lovemaking often raise objections. Fantastic sex is designed to be a mutual experience, and individual fantasy should always enhance, rather than detract from, mutual lovemaking.

On the other hand, certified sex therapist Barry McCarthy and his wife Emily have a different take on what constitutes healthy sexual fantasy.[4] The McCarthy's practice the Eastern sacred sexuality of Tantra and have been married over forty years and have co-authored eleven books on sexuality. They say the most frequent sexual fantasies involve a different partner, forced or forcing sex, group or threesome, being observed or observing someone else being sexual, or sex with someone of the same gender.

In other words, these fantasies emphasize people and scenarios that are totally outside the reality of your sex life. When asked if these erotic fantasies mean that a couple really wants to play them out in real life, they feel for the great majority of people, fantasies remain in a totally different domain than real-life behavior. In fact, they say, that is what makes the fantasy an erotic turn-on. For most couples, the result of playing out fantasies is disappointment.

A marriage counselor tells the story of a married Christian couple who fantasized regularly about a threesome with another woman. When the wife surprised her husband with a trip to a hotel room in which there was another woman paid to have sex with them, he could not go through with it. Fantasies no longer function as fantasies when they become reality, and most people realize that the erotic charge is much more intense in fantasy mode than in reality mode.

The McCarthy's believe the healthy function of sexual fantasy is to serve as a bridge to sexual desire and as a means to enhance arousal and orgasm. The key for healthy sexuality is to regard erotic fantasies as a bridge to intimate, interactive sexuality whether mutual or personal.

Sexual fantasy, like any other aspect of sexuality, can also be unhealthy. The McCarthy's say the most common problem is when fantasy acts as a wall instead of a bridge to sabotage couple sex. This is a special trap for males who fall into a sexual life of high eroticism, high shame, and secrecy—a powerful and destructive combination—over a variant arousal pattern, often prompted by Internet porn. Compulsive sex is not healthy sex.

When comparing either the Rosenau or McCarthy standard to the survey response, we see an immediate problem. Only one out of ten couples fantasize together, while three out of ten (and I suspect our survey number skews low—the McCarthy's research says seven out of ten) say they fantasize individually during couple sex. This certainly indicates a lack of honesty and communication, which is essential for an intimate sexual relationship.

Creating fantasies together (by this I mean fantasies

that lead to oneness with each other) adds variety, spice and romance to the sexual relationship. Instead of focusing on displeasing physical or emotional characteristics of your lover, instead fantasize about aspects that you find erotic and enticing. "We live in a world that glorifies youth, uncommitted sex, and bodies that require a ridiculous amount of self-serving time in the gym. Let's turn that around. Let's reaffirm the bodies of women who have generously and selflessly produced life for one, two, three, or more babies. Let's appreciate those men who work hard to support their families and who don't have time to stop off at the gym and lift weights because they're eager to get home and play with their kids."[5]

Moving from physical to emotional sexual affirmation leads to a sensual pathway toward mutual intimacy. This holistic approach provides the foundation to transcend beyond the sexual realm and into the sacred realm. We will talk much more about this in the last chapters. But for now, in order to experience this sort of spiritual transcendence, there must be mutual communication, awareness, and affirmation in sexual fantasy and sexual intercourse. When two lovers become physically and emotionally as one, a pathway opens that leads to the promise of spiritual oneness with each other and ultimately, to God.

Just as there are appropriate times for conventional sex, "quickies," and prolonged sexual encounters, there are appropriate times for utilizing differing degrees and types of sexual fantasy.

The Gift of Imagination

Routine dulls our perceptions. Anxiety makes us listless. Life becomes mundane and time hastens by. But imagination gives us breathtaking wonder.

Renowned physicist Albert Einstein once said, "Imagination is more important than knowledge. For knowledge is limited to all we now know and understand, while imagination embraces the entire world, and all there ever will be to know and understand." Our sexuality should not be bound by time and space. Rather, engaging the power of mutual imagination in sexual intimacy should send us soaring in the heavenlies, wild and free.

In today's world of quick-fixes, "seven steps to this and five steps to that" thinking, imagination has gone hungry, gone wanting; been stepped out, educated out, spanked out, and churched out—of our sexuality, our lives, our hearts. But look deep inside. Emerson comments, "If we can touch the imagination, we serve others...", not if we touch "their" imagination, but if we touch "the" imagination. God didn't make the imagination some small, human thing. It is larger than any single person, indeed, larger than any couple.

Without imagination, there is no understanding. But with it, there is every possibility we can imagine and more. It is power. It is potential. It is transcendent. It is wonder. It is replete with unexpected gifts. Unless we use our imagination, we are not *fully alive*. Wendell Berry says it this way: "The imagination is our way into the divine Imagination, permitting us to see wholly—as whole and holy—what we perceive to be scattered, as order what we perceive as random."[6] Imagine the possibilities if we expanded the power of our imagination to utilize sexual fantasy as a bridge to a deeper and exciting relationship with our lover and with God.

6.

the lie about sexual equality

"You don't have to be anti-man to be pro-woman."
Jane Galvin Lewis

When it comes to promoting full equality of the sexes, religion has a decidedly mixed reputation. Organized religion's treatment of women throughout the ages has been little different than secular culture. In general, religious women have derived their identity through males and are most often prized for their reproductive capabilities. A study of Mary, the mother of Jesus, reveals a figure that has been socially and sexually constructed (primarily by men) in such a way that her traditional titles of handmaid of the Lord, virgin, and mother have come to be controlling images in the Christian feminine ideal.[1]

Granted, I understand religion is only one of the vehicles of sexual inequality. The true origin of inequality is sin. In Genesis 5:1-2, God created man in His image, "male and female"—*before* the separation of Eve out of the body of Adam. Genesis makes this clear when God *describes* (not prescribes as many evangelical/conservatives have interpreted the text) what happens to relationships between men and women because of sin. When mankind (male and female) rejects God's rule, we become self-protective and self-centered.

God describes that as a result of sin, man will "rule over" the woman and the woman will have a "desire for the man." Van Leewan calls this "domination and enmeshment."[2] Men will seek power over women in order to dominate, and women will submit to it at any cost in order to maintain a relationship. Her "desire" will be for the man rather than for her own God-given authentic and individual personhood. Women throughout history have demonstrated this giving up of themselves for relationship by putting aside their gifts and calling, or tragically, submitting to abuse of all kinds— all to keep the man.

But scripture makes it very clear this was not God's plan. It is precisely because of the equality of the sexes, that Adam's unitive poem in Gen. 2:23 is followed immediately by the description of marriage, "For this reason a man will leave his father and mother and be united to his wife, and they will become *one flesh*" (2:24). Man and woman together were given the task of ruling (shared dominion) the world and multiplying. Only after sin was this distorted, which set the tone for stereotypes and inequality throughout history.

The apostle Paul (used by some religious leaders to promote a hierarchical view of men over women) wrote definitively in 2 Corinthians 5:17-20 that *anyone*—man or woman—who is in Christ is a new creation and *all* are given "the ministry of reconciliation as an ambassador for Christ."

However, it was not until the advent of the feminist movement (the first wave was in the 1920s and the second wave was from the 60s to the 80s) that women gradually begin to gain recognition as equals. Many religions, including most Sacramentalist denominations, such as the Roman Catholic Church, as well as the "biblically inerrant" denominations such as the Conservative Baptist Association still do not accept women for ordination into the ministry and continue to exclude them from major leadership positions. As recently as June of 2000, the Southern Baptist Convention raised considerable controversy by an addition to its *Baptist Faith and Message* concerning the sexes.

To many, the language of the amendment seems to place women in a subservient position. Judge for yourself:

> *The husband and wife are of equal worth to God, since both are created in God's image. The marriage relationship models the way God relates to His people. A husband is to love his wife as Christ loved the church. He has the God-given responsibility to provide for, to protect, and to lead his family. A wife is to submit herself graciously to the servant leadership of her husband even as the church willingly submits to the headship of Christ. She, being in the image of God as is her husband and thus equal to him, has the God-given responsibility to respect her husband and to serve him as helper in managing the household and nurturing the next generation.[3]*

The Bible, in contrast to religion, is replete with examples of teaching and history that are contrary to the pattern of objectification of women. Rev. Candie Blankman points out that even though the Old Testament law seems archaic and oppressive, to the 21st century mind, it actually moved women toward more equal treatment. For instance, in ancient Hebrew culture, women were property. They had no status apart from the husband or head of household that owned them. However, the Old Testament law insisted that when a woman was put out or divorced, she was given "papers" to identify who she was and why she was outside the common relationship of wife, concubine, or slave/household worker.

This was a huge step forward for women, particularly when you consider this brutal story. In the book of Judges chapter nineteen, a Levite, his concubine and his servant were traveling from Bethlehem back to their homes in the hills of Ephraim. During the night a mob, with homosexual rape in mind, surrounded the house in which they were staying and demanded the Levite be sent out. The host offered them his virgin daughter and the concubine instead; eventually the poor concubine was thrown to the mob. At dawn the Levite found her either dead or comatose on the doorstep. He took her inside and cut her up into 12 pieces. Perhaps because of behavior such as this, the Old Testament law also put limitations on the kind of horrifying treatment that women could be given.

Abraham was instructed to actually listen to his wife Sarah. Deborah was designated as a judge of Israel. Miriam led alongside Moses and Aaron. Though incremental at times, there was still movement forward.

Rev. Blankman goes on to recount a remarkable fact in the Exodus story—the single most significant historical memory of the Israelites—the first five people named in the record are women, including two mid-wives, Puah and Shiphrah. Not even the most powerful man in the story is named. He is just referred to as the Pharaoh. But five women are cited and identified as the most significant players in God's story of redemption.

Jesus welcomed women into His cadre of male disciples and treated them with an unusually high degree of respect. The encounter with the Samaritan woman at the well and His relationship with Mary Magdalene provide examples of precedent-setting approaches to the female-male relationship. Jesus also allowed women to be testimony bearers of His resurrection in a time when women could not even be used as witnesses in a court of law. He was simply living out what was originally intended from the beginning.

In Galatians 3, Paul, who usually gets tagged with the title of male chauvinist, gives the quintessential statement of equality when he says that in Christ there is neither Jew nor Greek, slave or free, male or female, but all are one (equal) in Christ. So we see that in the community and kingdom where Jesus reigns and rules—equality is for all.

Now would be a good time to explain that during my years of research for the historical context of this book, two overarching themes emerged. Those issues were first, *female inequality* and the resulting dehumanization of women, and second, a hierarchical alpha leadership of *religious control.*

In culture and religion, women have long been objectified and despite valiant feminist efforts, this mindset of dehumanization persists. Sexual objectification has been defined as the separating of a person's body, body parts, or sexual functions, from his or her person, reducing them to the status of mere instruments.[4] The sad reality is that at some levels of consciousness, most religions and men view women as objects to be repressed and controlled. It seems that this false division of body and soul permeates every aspect of our lives.

The media have played a particularly insidious role in promoting the dehumanization of sexual objectification. Studies have characterized sexual objectification by the media as instances in which the focus is on isolated body parts, such as a bare stomach, buttocks, cleavage, a bare chest, or reproductive capabilities in the absence of a focus on the rest of the person. The general conclusion of these studies is that the media often focus on the body and appearance as the most important components of sexual desirability.[5]

Only by understanding the unity and diversity of the sexes do we begin to fathom male and female distinctions and the mystery inherent in sexual equality and communion. Dr. Louis Markos describes this paradox of unity and diversity as, "a fittedness of the sexes; both are distinct, both are equally created in the image of God, and yet both belong together."[6]

There is danger in viewing a human being as a *thing*, rather than the miraculous interrelation of body and soul that God originally created. Unfortunately, it is the female sex that has suffered the majority of harm from sexual, self, and religious objectification. Let's first examine each area of objectification and finish by exploring the hopeful possibilities that God's original plan of unity within diversity has to offer.

Objectification of women occurs primarily within three interrelated dimensions:

- *Sexual Objectification* — is characterized by cultural expectations and values that are communicated in myriad ways, including through the media. Our culture has been infused with sexualized representations of girls and women, suggesting that such sexual objectification is good and normal.

- *Self-Objectification* — occurs when women treat and experience themselves as sexual objects.[7] If women learn that sexualized behavior and appearance are approved of and rewarded by society and by the people (e.g., peers and religion) whose opinions matter most to them, they are likely to internalize these standards, thus engaging in self-objectification.

- *Religious Objectification* — occurs when women are treated as, and encouraged to be, sexual objects by religion. This happens by treating a woman as a religious thing. The working definition of "thing" is that which is one dimensional, incapable of independent thought, autonomous decision-making and self-sufficiency.

Sexual Objectification

Perhaps the most pervasive form of objectification is sexual and therefore deserves a closer look. The different components of sexual objectification set it apart from healthy sexuality, which is an important part of both physical and mental health. A healthy sexuality fosters intimacy, bonding, and shared pleasure, and involves mutual respect between consenting partners.[8] In contrast, sexual objectification occurs when:

- A person's value comes only from his or her sexual appeal or behavior, to the exclusion of other characteristics;

- A person is held to a standard that equates physical attractiveness (narrowly defined) with being sexy;

- A person is sexually objectified—that is, made into a thing for others' sexual use, rather than seen as a person with the capacity for independent action and decision-making.

All three conditions need not be present; each one on its own can be an indication of sexual objectification. Anyone (girls, boys, men, and women) can be sexualized. A central assumption of sexual objectification is that women in particular, exist in a culture in which their bodies are "looked at, evaluated, and always potentially objectified."[9]

Media

Throughout U.S. culture, and particularly in mainstream media, women and girls are depicted in a sexualizing manner. It is important to consider this staggering statistic: the average child views over six hours of media per day. The Kaiser Family Foundation (2003) reports that 68% of children have a TV in their bedroom. These massive doses of media among youth create the potential for prolonged exposure to portrayals that sexualize women and teach girls that women are sexual objects.

In their analysis of sexual harassment on prime-time programming, Grauerholz and King report a focus on the denigration of women that alluded to their sexuality and lack of intellect and that objectified their bodies.[10] Of the episodes analyzed, 84 percent contained at least one incident of sexual harassment. The most frequent acts were sexist comments in which a wide variety of deprecating words were used to describe women (e.g., *broad, bimbo, dumb ass chick, toots, fox, babe, blondie*). The next most frequent occurrences were verbal sexual comments. These comments typically focused on women's bodies or body parts, especially breasts, which were referred to as *jugs, boobs, knockers, hooters, cookware,* and *canned goods.* The third most common category was body language and generally involved men or adolescent boys leering at women or girls.

In total, researchers report that approximately 78 percent of the harassment focused on demeaning terms for women or on the sexual objectification of their bodies. This means that adolescents are learning how to behave, interact, speak, dress, and conceptualize themselves based on shows such as these. Tops are getting tighter. Jeans are getting lower. Skirts are getting shorter and the conversations that adolescents are having these days sometimes borders on pornographic. Scary isn't it?

It is important to remember that these shows are where adolescents learn much of their behavior (cultural and sexual), language, interactions and self-worth. If you find this hard to believe, answer this. What parent, no matter how nurturing, is spending six hours every day with their child?

Music Videos & Lyrics

Ever since the advent of MTV, viewers have been eager to visualize their favorite songs and be entertained. As our senses have been slightly dulled by the constant barrage of sex in the media, the artists and producers constantly have to push the envelope to boost sales and maintain the audience's interest by means of shock value. That means more sex, more visual stimulation, crude lyrics, and more objectification.

The lyrics of many recent popular songs sexually objectify women or refer to them in highly degrading ways, or both. Some examples include the following:

- *"So blow me bitch I don't rock for cancer/I rock for the cash and the topless dancers."* (Kid Rock, 1998)

- *"Don'tcha wish your girlfriend was hot like me?"* (Pussycat Dolls, 2005)

- *"That's the way you like to f*** . . . rough sex make it hurt, in the garden all in the dirt."* (Ludacris, 2000)

- *"I tell the hos all the time, Bitch get in my car."* (50 Cent, 2005)

- *"Ho shake your ass."* (Ying Yang Twins, 2003)

In music videos, sexually objectifying images of women constitute a large portion of the prolific sexual content. Women, more frequently than men, are presented in provocative and revealing clothing, and typically serve as decorative objects that dance and pose and do not play any instruments. They are often displayed in ways that emphasize their bodies, body parts, facial features, and sexual readiness. Even though in female singer's videos, men are also objectified, we somehow don't seem to notice, because the majority of these types of videos are by male singers.

Studies found that over half of the videos featured a woman portrayed exclusively as a decorative sexual object. In the videos analyzed, almost 40 percent of women wore revealing clothing, compared with four percent of men. A more recent analysis of the most popular music videos on Black Entertainment Television (BET) found sexual imagery in over 80 percent of the videos; the two most frequently occurring sexual behaviors were sexual objectification and women dancing sexually. Seventy-one percent of women in these videos were dressed in provocative clothing or wore no clothing at all causing the television network to employ a censor bar because of FCC regulations.[11]

Movies

Nudity is not unlike violence in movies in that subsequent movies have more and more of it, as if to out-do any previous movie in its genre. We want graphic and we want passion. We're a culture thirsty for visual stimulation and we prove our devotion by record-breaking box office sales.

One of the patterns that has been studied in movies is the disproportional presence of nudity. In R-rated movies of the last two decades, instances of female nudity were reported to exceed those of male nudity by a 4 to 1 ratio.[12] An increasing number of movies with sexual themes have plots that appeal primarily to teen and young adult audiences. And adolescents (lots of them) are at the front of the ticket line. They constitute the largest demographic segment of moviegoers. If you don't believe this, try going to your local cinema any Friday or Saturday evening. At my theatre, adolescents routinely purchase tickets for PG-rated movies and after showing their ticket, simply walk into the R-rated movie of their choice.

These R-rated movies contain sex scenes on a regular basis that would have been subjugated to seedy adults-only XXX theatres only a few short years ago. Recent movies such as *Black Snake Moan* and *A History of Violence* are two examples of many that contain brutal rape and mistreatment of female characters; these films are a short walk across the hallway for any enterprising adolescent.

Another notable trend is the near absence of female characters in the top-grossing motion pictures and in G-rated movies. A study by the research firm Kelly and Smith evaluated the 101 top-grossing G-rated films (including

Disney) from 1990 to 2004. Of the over 4,000 characters in these films, 75% overall were male, 83% of characters in crowds were male, 83% of narrators were male, and 72% of speaking characters were male.[13]

This gross under-representation of women or girls in films with family-friendly content reflects a missed opportunity to present a broad spectrum of women in roles that are nonsexualized. It also leaves a younger generation lacking healthy role models and worse, it cheats us of the opportunity for better role models in the future.

Magazines

Sex sells. And magazines know it. They grab your attention weekly with airbrushed pictures of your favorite celebrity and promise tips on how to please a man or how to make a woman beg for more sex. It's not too surprising that even women's magazines objectify women in the images they show and the tips they give. Women's magazines generally give hints to women on how to improve themselves and make themselves more desirable in the eyes of a man. Men's magazines, however, focus on how to seduce women. In both cases, a woman is seen as a sexual item, able to be seduced, but never complete without the desire from a man.

Women are repeatedly encouraged to look and dress in specific ways to look sexy for men. They are also bombarded with advertisements to use products in order to be more attractive to and desired by men. This phenomenon has been labeled "costuming for seduction."[14]

These studies document that attracting the attention of males by looking "hot" and "sexy" is the point of many of the articles, text, cover lines, ads, and photographs. Repeated attempts are made, in the form of advice about hairstyles, cosmetics, clothing, diet, and exercise, to remake the reader as an object of male desire.

Sports Media

Sports are certainly not immune to sexualization. Several targeted studies of specific media genres, sports, or sporting events have documented the frequency with which female athletes are sexualized. One study found that only 10% of the photographs in *Sports Illustrated* were of female athletes. And five percent of those were "pornographic or sexually suggestive," such as women dressed provocatively or photographed in such a way as to focus solely on sexual attributes (e.g., photograph framed on an athlete's breasts).

Less than one percent of the photographs of men fell into this category. Sixty-six percent of the photographs of men showed them actively engaged in a sport versus 34% of the photographs of women. Representations of women in *Sports Illustrated for Women* were only slightly better; 56% of photographs of women in *SIW* depicted them actively engaged in sports, and 2% were pornographic.[15] This suggests in a crude way that no matter how talented a female athlete is, she is only popular because she has a nice figure, perhaps a pretty face, and breasts.

Advertising

The sexual objectification of women is particularly prominent in the world of advertising. In prime-time television commercials, for example, women were twice more likely than men to be shown in a state of undress, to exhibit more "sexiness," and depicted as sexual objects. Alcohol is sold by young, curvaceous women on billboards and now even websites have turned to sex to sell, such as the ridiculous GoDaddy commercials during the Superbowl. The frequency with which young women and adult women are consistently and increasingly presented in sexualized ways in advertising, creates an environment in which being female becomes nearly synonymous with being a sexual object.

News stories over the last 25 years have documented ads—both successful and controversial—that have been debated and sometimes pulled because of their presentation of sexualized young girls. The Brooke Shields Calvin Klein jeans ad, and in more recent years, the Abercrombie and Fitch catalogue, the Calvin Klein child underwear ads, the Christina Aguilera Sketchers ads, and the "children" utilized in highly sexual fashion ads for Dolce & Gabbana are among some of the more risqué.

Such ads often take a star popular with teens and preteens and present her in highly sexualized poses. Some explicitly play up innocence as sexy, as in one of the Sketchers "naughty and nice" ads that featured Aguilera dressed as a schoolgirl in pigtails, with her shirt unbuttoned, licking a lollipop. One study concludes that the message from advertisers and the mass media to girls (as eventual women) is they should always be sexually available, always have sex on their minds, be willing to be dominated and even sexually aggressed against, and they will be gazed on as sexual objects.[16]

The evidence overwhelmingly demonstrates that women and girls are more likely than men and boys to be objectified and sexualized in a variety of media outlets (including television, magazines, sports media, and music videos), and in advertising. Portrayals of adult women provide girls with models they can use to fashion their own behaviors, self-concepts, and identities after. In this way, girls learn from a very young age that they are sexual objects, even before they truly know what sex is.

Self-Objectification

Self-objectification involves adopting a third-person perspective on the physical self and constantly assessing one's own body in an effort to conform to the culture's standards of attractiveness. A woman is a "good object" when she meets the salient cultural standard of "sexy." But this leads girls to evaluate and control their own bodies more in terms of their sexual desirability to others than in terms of their own desires, health, or competence.

There is ample evidence that self-objectification is common among girls and women. For example, one study found that girls as young as 12 years old placed greater emphasis on their body's appearance than on its ability. In addition, many studies have demonstrated that girls and women self-objectify much more than boys and men.[17]

Although influences on self-objectification might include a variety of interpersonal, social, cultural, and even biological factors such as physical strength, two aggressive purveyors of sexual objectification are religion and the mass media. Thus, it stands to reason that religion and media exposure high in sexual objectification can socialize women to objectify themselves as inferiors. Both young and adult women who continuously see others' sexuality objectified in religion and the media, seem prone to view themselves as objects to be looked at and used by others.

Likewise, self-objectification in a religious culture suggests that sexualization practices may function to keep women "in their place" as objects of beauty, art, and property, significantly limiting their ability to think freely and exert influence.

Religious Objectification

Both religious objectification and sexual objectification of women seem to be two threads in the same strand. That strand leads back to the three major Western religions—Christianity, Islam, and Judaism. As the thread unravels, there seems to be a direct correlation: The more conservative the sect or branch, the less equality for women.

These threads of objectification have turned women into a religious thing. Remember that one may define "thing" as one dimensional, incapable of independent thought, autonomous decision-making and self-sufficiency. Religious objectification is a consequence of the need for alpha male leadership to demonize and marginalize women to solidify the controlling power of the religious hierarchy.

Now, that's a lot of fancy words to say basically that the preachers and other religious heads got together and said, "Let's eliminate the competition (read: women) by convincing everyone that women are inferior, subservient and useful only for beauty, labor, and reproduction." The post-modern version of this imperative is "keep all women in their place by grouping them with other sexualized women in Bible Study cliques, as makers and teachers of children, and as pretty singers since they have nothing of value to offer religious male leadership who have been appointed as God's intermediaries."

In the end, the sexualization and objectification of women in religion teaches girls that as women, all they have to offer is their body and reproductive capabilities and therefore they should expend all their effort on appearances. When women are seen exclusively as sexualized beings rather than multi-dimensional persons with many interests, talents, and identities, men have difficulty relating to them on any other than surface level. This dramatically limits the opportunities men have to interact spiritually and intellectually with women, to create with them, to work together for higher causes (e.g., leadership), or to enjoy their company as equals. It also promotes unhealthy sexual relationships.

A Healthy Equality

This begs the question, how can a couple possibly enjoy complete respect and intimacy without acknowledging that each has a responsibility to allow the other to bring all that they are as *equal* human beings to the sexual experience? And, can a true recognition of simultaneous unity and division combined with an attitude of mutual reverence and respect provide the opportunity for both woman and man to see the face of God *in each other* through sacred sexuality?

First, to address the former question: A woman who has learned to fear negative evaluations of her body may be more focused on her partner's judgments of her than on her own desires, safety, and pleasure. Focusing critically and excessively on one's own appearance can limit the pleasure drawn from sexual experiences and can make it difficult for women to wholly engage. At the same time, a woman who has been socialized to separate from her inner feelings and experiences of arousal and desire may find it difficult to assert her desires or feel entitled to mutual satisfaction in sexual situations. She may instead opt to let events unfold based on her partner's wants and interests. I might note here that many men are socialized to internalize emotions and feelings as well, so they are also often troubled in expressing wants and desires and emotions, especially during sex.

This perceived inequality creates an unhealthy sexual and spiritual relationship. It is impossible for the woman (or man) to find a spiritual awareness or completeness when sexual communion takes place on uneven ground. It cannot be stressed enough; a healthy sacred sexual relationship requires a paradox of unity and diversity, a fittedness of the sexes; both distinct, both equally created in the image of God, and both belonging together.

Second, sacred sexuality offers women important practical and psychological alternatives to the values conveyed by popular culture. When healthy couples through their personal sacred practices, communicate the message that other characteristics such as emotional and spiritual intelligence, are just as important as sexuality, they help to counteract the strong and prevalent message that only sexuality makes a person interesting, desirable, or valuable.

By insisting that both sexes be allowed freedom—not pushed into a self-objectification mindset, a haven develops where women and men can flourish as equals. In addition, religious institutions should be encouraged to offer open and honest classes and seminars in sacred sexuality so that healthy and unhealthy couples can enjoy the support, not condemnation, of their church or parish.

One of my favorite writers, Madeline L'Engle says it this way, "I am a female of the species, man. Genesis is very explicit that it takes both male and female to make the image of God, and that the generic word, man, includes both. *God created man in His own image, male and female.* That is scripture, therefore I refuse to be timid about being part of mankind. We of the female sex are half of mankind, and it is cowardly to resort to he/she, him/her, or even worse, android words. I have a hunch that those who would do so have forgotten their rightful heritage."[18]

7.

the lie about yada, yada, yada

"Sex is everywhere except in sex."
Roland Barthes

No, I'm not talking about a *Seinfeld* episode. The Hebrew word "Yada" means "to know." It further means to have an intimate and interactive relationship with its subject.[1] This word is used with great reverence in the Bible to denote God's love for mankind, and for man's desire to know God. The sense of the word is profound; it does not imply a casual relationship, but a deep and intimate relationship between God and man. The same word is also used to describe the way a man and wife should know one another. In this sense, "yada, yada, yada" might be understood as an ignorant disparagement of profound relationships, demeaning the word into a phrase that signifies nothing important.

But ironically, it was religion, not *Seinfeld* that first demeaned the word Yada. For fifteen hundred years, from Augustine to the present day, religion has taught that original sin corrupted our sexuality. We have ingrained in our psyche that we are "sinners saved by grace." Celebrated religious leader Martin Luther said that, since Eden, sexual intercourse was "horribly marred" by the "hideousness inherent in our flesh, namely, the bestial desire and lust," and that sex, even in marriage, was never free from sin.

But what if this word "yada" offers a key—perhaps *the* key—to unlocking the mystery that lies at the heart of marriage, and therefore at the heart of sexuality, and most importantly at the heart of transcendent intimacy and interaction with God? What if ancient Eastern sacred sexual practices represent an ideal basis for a reimagination of modern erotic Western sexuality? What if we really believed that sex is sacred and not a sin? What if Colossians 1:22, "But now he has reconciled you by Christ's physical body through death to present you holy in his sight, *without blemish and free from accusation*", were really true?[2]

The Ladder of Yada

The Yada sexual time is a tactile path and uses touch as the primary sensory avenue for awareness and focus. The sexual sensation is the most evocative and powerful tactile sense man can experience. And when that sensation results in climax, we experience a time of Yada, or union with our partner and with God.

It is fascinating to note that in the original Greek, climax means "a ladder to heaven." Through sex, we have been given the opportunity to *directly* experience our ascent to the heavens described in Ephesians 2:6.[3] A further understanding of Yada clarifies that climax refers not to a single given moment at the top, but rather to the duration of the climb. Climax is best understood as durations of time. The journey is the destination.

Yada comprises the extraordinary invitation to re-enact the original experiences of creation on a very personal and erotic level, while at the same time mysteriously transcending heaven on a sacred level. I should point out that Yada sex is not just ordinary conventional sex. Conventional sex can be for procreation (making babies), an expression of love (reward), for simple pleasure (a "quickie"), and to relieve anxiety or tension (release). All of these types of sex are wonderful and should not be minimized.

However, Yada sex requires a very different mindset, a mutual commitment worthy of careful planning. This is especially true if you have small children, pets, careers, or other barriers that hinder an extended time of uninterrupted privacy. I would recommend setting aside at least a three-hour time slot to maximize the Yada experience. A time of mutual advance preparation will also be required—and can made be really fun as well. The importance of regular times of Yada cannot be overstated. Even if the frantic pace of Westernized society allows you only one time a month, make it a priority. You'll thank me.

Characteristics of Yada

First, let's look at four structural characteristics of Yada.

1. A simultaneous unity and division with an attitude of reverence and respect for each other and God is celebrated.

2. Sexual intercourse is conducted utilizing the five senses (sight, hearing, touch, smell, taste).

3. Orgasm is not the goal.

4. The desired outcome of Yada sexual activity is to produce a new and transcendent awareness.

The first point above is perhaps the most challenging and rewarding aspect of exchanging life in Yada relationships. In fact, relationship is the heart of Yada. It brings us face to face with our humanness. One of the greatest challenges a person encounters is that of growing together in an extended relationship with a mate and with God.

Relationships are extraordinarily complicated but by committing and recommitting to the relationship, maintaining an attitude of reverence toward your partner, exchanging love, recognizing unity and division, and showing kindness, you are practicing a transcendent sexuality of the highest order. You are finding the extraordinary in the ordinary.

Second, Yada also employs a multi-sensory approach to the sexual experience. It is important to take time to savor the unfamiliar aspects of the familiar. Third, even though I highlight a "time of orgasm," it is important to remember that orgasm is not the goal. It can be a glorious peak in the course of the journey, but the journey is most important.

To illustrate the progression to the fourth point, let me tell you about my experience in leading multi-day backpacking expeditions into the wilderness. As we began our journey, inevitably both men and women would find themselves rushing down the trail to the first destination. When I would arrive at the campsite sometimes hours after them, they would ask what had happened to me. This provided a perfect teaching moment to emphasize the short and valuable time we were able to spend in the wilderness was about enjoying the journey, *not* the destination. The next morning, I would watch as everyone visibly took a deep breath and began to notice the beauty that encompassed them.

Our western culture demands a frenetic pace. It is important to take time to acclimate and breathe deeply before plunging into Yada. If we somehow manage to slow down, the opportunity for a new awareness presents itself. We begin to notice and savor the positive spiritual, emotional and physical aspects of our mate and perhaps, in those nuances, we will transcend the earth for a few precious moments and glimpse the face of God.

I believe that everyone has the potential to enjoy transcendent sexuality by celebrating the following three steps or "times" of Yada.

A Time of Excitement, Senses, and Motivation

Renowned sex researchers Masters and Johnson outline four phases they call the sexual response cycle: excitement, plateau, orgasmic peaking, and resolution. I have taken the liberty to combine the first two phases into an extended excitement phase.

In Yada, sexuality is not orgasm-oriented, though orgasm may take place. It emphasizes and prolongs the excitement phase. When excitement is prolonged, the two other phases—orgasm and wonder—are much more profound and occur automatically. Also, extending the excitement time intimately relates to the fourth foundational characteristic of Yada sexual practice, that of a new and transcendent awareness.

In contrast to most Western sex researchers, the Yada ladder takes the excitement phase and prolongs it. This extended excitement time is usually followed by a strong orgasm (with or without ejaculation), and then a highly contemplative time of wonder.

The first advantage of prolonging the excitement time, focusing on the means rather than the ends, is that it engages the soul. The three aspects of the soul; the head, personality, and heart have time to engage and gradually begin to recreate the original experience of Eden. They begin to "experience the simultaneous unity and division, oneness and *'two-ness'* of male and female. The first poem recorded in the Hebrew Bible occurs in Genesis 1:27, which the New International Version correctly prints in poetic form:

> *So God created man in his own image,*
> *in the image of God he created him;*
> *male and female he created them.*

Here too we find the same fittedness of the sexes; both are distinct, both are equally created in the image of God, and yet both belong together in transcendent union."[4]

The second advantage to prolonging the excitement time is that it engages the body. A form of physical response occurs in both men and women. This response is a product of glandular secretions. The more the excitement phase is prolonged, the more the glands secrete.

For example, under certain circumstances when a woman's breasts are stimulated, the reflex goes straight to the pituitary gland, which then releases a hormone that flows through the bloodstream down to the uterus, causing a contraction. That is why many women can have orgasms from breast stimulation alone.

A similar physical response happens in men. The prolonging of excitement and the release of hormones and endorphins into the body produce a new awareness that can persist for some time, even after orgasm takes place. This produces a very powerful and healthy natural euphoria that can be beneficial for relieving anxiety and improving mood.

One problem with this prolonged time of excitement is that it can lead to anxiety on the man's part concerning premature ejaculation. It should be re-emphasized that the ejaculation is not the goal in Yada but it is okay if it happens at any time during the journey. The participants should practice the lost art of relaxation throughout the excitement time and the time of wonder. Again, focus on the excitement time, not the orgasm.

Important in this approach is the understanding that the excitement phase has its own ebb and flow, so for men, the external sign for arousal (erection) is not nearly so important. So again, relax. Each Yada time of excitement is unique and has its own particular value, and it is not the opening act before the main event. Thus, there is nothing to lose—no success, no failure, only the transcendence of the experience itself. This concept seems easy to understand intellectually, but it takes time to absorb it and live it with our Western mindset, where we are trained from an early age to be goal-oriented beings.

The excitement time is also the "senses" time, and truly experiencing it involves becoming aware of and immersed in a spiritual energy that few in the West ever consider or recognize. A transcendent union (a new awareness) with your partner is a spiritual state that is characterized by Yada sexuality.

This transcendent union comes from a prolonging of the excitement time. The spiritual couple employs the mystery and beauty of their bodies and souls to sensually move toward the experience of sexual communion.

During this time, utilization of all five senses can be employed. The sense of *touch* can be used by prolonged stimulation of the body through massage and extended caresses of the body utilizing knowledge of primary, secondary, and tertiary erogenous zones. Indeed, the entire surface of the skin becomes an erogenous zone. Mutual masturbation can also be enjoyed, with each partner masturbating in front of the other or by masturbating your partner, but being careful not to over-stimulate.

Your body's erogenous zone can generally be divided into three different types:

1. Primary (first-degree) erogenous zone: The lips, genitals, and nipples. These areas include the anus, penis, vaginal lips, and inside the outer part of the vagina. They are rich in nerves and the nerve endings are very close to the surface of the skin. These areas are very responsive to touch.

2. Secondary (second-degree) erogenous zone: Parts that have a sparse amount of hair and are often found in the regions next to the third-degree areas such as the neck, ears, and abdomen. These parts are not as sensitive as the primary erogenous zone, but are more sensitive than the areas covered by hair.

3. Tertiary (third-degree) erogenous zone: The areas of the skin that are covered with hair—your arms, legs, parts of the chest, and so forth. These areas have fewer and more dispersed nerve endings, so

they are the least erogenous. Nevertheless, the hair follicles' ends, down under the skin, help stimulate the nerve endings that are buried near them.[5]

Looking each other in the eyes can enhance the sense of *sight*, which foreshadows the time of transcendence when we hope to see God face-to-face. True Yada demands eye contact. Sight also includes carefully chosen aesthetic surroundings, candlelight, and silky clothing or lingerie.

The sense of *smell* benefits from carefully chosen natural incense and perfume with each participant's pheromonal preferences in mind.[6] The most effective fragrance is one that mixes well with your own body chemistry. Try sampling a perfume beforehand and allowing it to merge with your own body oils for several minutes before smelling it. Then once it has had time to mix with your own scent, make sure it is one you both enjoy.

A scent of an associative memory can also trigger romantic feelings. For example, the scent of a certain perfume or cologne that your partner has already used and to which you are attracted can trigger a pleasing response.

Listening to your favorite romantic music, reading poetry, exchanging whispers, sexual fantasy and other verbal affirmations, stimulates the sense of *hearing*. This is one of the most important senses to shield from distraction so that's why you need extended time alone.

The sense of *taste* can savor the taste of food, wine, kisses to the mouth, skin and oral sex. It is unfortunate that many religious people have attached a negative stigma to oral sex, believing it is a "dirty" and sinful practice.

Nothing could be further from the truth. We have let culture and religion negatively affect one of the most intimate and interactive of the sexual acts. Internationally known evangelical psychologist, Dr. Kevin Leman in his wonderful book *Sheet Music*, says that if God were to give him a magic wand, he would wave it over couples all over the world and grant them a greater freedom and sense of exploration.

He goes on to say the Bible is silent on oral sex, which says to most Bible scholars it must be okay. He continues, "Think about it—if kissing someone on the lips is okay then why is a kiss anywhere else 'immoral'? It certainly isn't a matter of hygiene. To put it bluntly, when a woman kisses a man's freshly washed penis, the woman's mouth has far more germs than the man's penis. So, if you're truly concerned about hygiene, forget mouth-to-mouth kissing and go straight to oral sex."[7] Much more could obviously be mentioned here, but instead, I encourage a vivid use of imagination.

The more clutter we have in our lives, the more difficult it is to employ Yada. Constant distraction, whether physical (not being completely alone or able to enjoy the time without mental distractions) or sensual (such as distracting noises) can hinder the ability to transcend earth with our partner in this prolonged time of excitement.

Another key characteristic of the excitement time is that of motivation. As we spend prolonged time selflessly getting to know our partner in an intimate way as a lover, we are impregnated with grace, which enables us to choose and act with a transcendent motivation. Yada is a time of grace—not judgment.

We must also actively study scripture to understand Christ's motivation in order to imitate Him in our own sexual communion. While that might sound foreign at first and hard to understand, in practice, it's very simple. As we serve our lover by sacrificing our own needs, we gradually come to live out our sexuality with a new motivation—that of Christ. The natural connection between pleasure and motivation will be replaced with a desire to help our lover in their journey to transcendent intimacy. This will lead to a heightened sense of kindness to one another.

A proper motivation will cause us to develop a life of discipline and simplicity. We should discipline our selfish shortcomings. Selfishness causes us to fixate upon our own satisfaction and ignore our partner's needs. We must spend

time getting to know the one who would have us as lover.
As we share intercourse, by alternately giving and receiving,
the Spirit consummates our love and flows through us and
influences everyone we meet.

A Time of Orgasm, Spirit, and Reliance

Walt Whitman vividly describes our next step in the poem,
"The Body Electric":

> *Hair, bosom, hips, bend of legs,*
> *Negligent falling hands all*
> *Diffused, mine too diffused,*
> *Ebb stung by the flow and flow stung*
> *by the ebb, love-flesh swelling*
> *And deliciously aching,*
> *Limitless limpid jets of love hot and*
> *Enormous, quivering jelly of*
> *Love, white-blow and delirious nice,*
> *Bridegroom night of love working*
> *Surely and softly into the*
> *prostrate dawn,*
> *Undulating into the willing and yielding*
> *Day,*
> *Lost in the cleave of the clasping and*
> *Sweet-fleshed day.*

The time of orgasm described so beautifully is the peak
of the sexual response cycle, characterized by an intense
sensation of pleasure. For men, generally a description of an
explosion of fireworks precedes a powerful rush of feelings.
Women can also experience intense orgasms. They often
describe their feelings as waves of pleasure accompanied by
a flooding sensation that permeates the body. Ultimately, for
both sexes, orgasm occurs in the mind and is simultaneously
accompanied by a pleasurable physical response. Maybe
that's why my friend Betty, a Christian sex therapist, says,

"Each of us are responsible for our own orgasm." When all is said and done, the response is up to each of us as individuals.

In Western culture, the pre-eminence of the orgasm has been exaggerated. It seems important to reiterate that Yada is not about the destination, but the journey. No evaluation or critique should be given at any time—only guidance and encouragement. The complete happiness of each partner reigns supreme, regardless of orgasm.

Many times, however, an orgasm for one or the other, in some cases both, will be desired. In this case, the key word is reliance. Open and honest communication and mutual reliance combine to produce exquisite results. As mentioned earlier, "almost two-thirds of women cannot achieve orgasm without direct stimulation of the clitoris." The woman must rely on manual, oral or mechanical stimulation to provide orgasm, and her partner must rely on adequate communication and guidance to provide the most enjoyable experience.

In the orgasmic time, Yada provides an opportunity for more than physical pleasure. Embracing spiritual communion leads to an awareness that in the orgasmic moment, a moment of transcendence can take place. That moment is literally a journey to a new awareness of your partner and of God by means of a spiritual and selfless experience.

Imagine at the brink of orgasm, upon reaching the "point of no return," you purposefully focus your spirit, by faith, upon a transcendent awareness of your partner or God. I have already stated that the head determines how we experience orgasm. It does so by forming concepts and images through imagination. But what if we could move beyond a conceptual orgasm, which is partial at best, to a new type of complete spiritual orgasm called faith?

What causes the head to move from a *reliance* on concepts and images to a reliance on faith? It is a new and pure awareness. As we gradually practice this transformation of understanding, we move from a natural awareness to a spiritual awareness. We no longer look at our partner and God as merely concepts and images; rather, we see them in all their completeness and wildness.

Sound impossible? I don't think it is. I *do* acknowledge it is a gradual and even painful process of moving beyond our natural awareness to a more complete spiritual awareness—a more intense spiritual awareness than we ever imagined possible. This purification of awareness entails what it means to experience spiritual communion in a true *knowledge* of your lover. I believe that a mutual discovery of the nuances of this knowledge, Yada, with the Spirit as our guide can lead to the very face of God. Jesus said emphatically that the pure in heart shall *see* God. What an orgasmic thought!

A Time of Wonder, Life, and Perception

The ascent of the ladder is not yet complete. There remains a time of wonder. It is that time when no matter the financial or family problems, no matter the turmoil that pervades the world, for a few brief moments, "all is right in the world." As we collapse in sweaty euphoria, we together realize a time of transcendent wonder. There dawns a realization that we have indeed been granted the privilege to see the face of a holy God.

As we gently touch and affirm each other, sharing awareness and basking in the wonder of the experience, we realize that we have spiritually exchanged life. A characteristic that embodies the time of wonder is the creation and re-creation *of life*. God designed sexual communion so that it holds the possibility of a man and woman miraculously creating physical life, that of a child, mirroring the relationship and mystery of the Holy Trinity. It also celebrates the original experience of life when at the beginning of time "man and woman he created them," mirroring our relationship to the incarnate Christ who is the Word made flesh. And, wonder of wonders, it celebrates the possibility of a daily life of completion and wholeness, mirroring our relationship with the Holy Spirit.

Henry David Thoreau said, "It's not what you look at, it's what you see that counts." Many times we hurry through life looking but never seeing. It is a matter of perception. The time of wonder provides an opportunity to reflect upon the mystery of transcendent sexual communion. It is a *perception* of the miraculous exchange of life that has just taken place. We have been granted the joy of Yada, knowing one another and God in a sensual and transcendent way. And somehow in that knowing, we have glimpsed the face of God and felt His intimate and complete love for us.

The immortal poet John Donne describes it this way:

> *Batter my heart, three person'd God; for you*
> *As yet but knocke, breathe, shine, and seeke to mend;*
> *That I may rise, and stand, o'erthrow mee, 'and bend*
> *Your force, to breake, blowe, burn and make me new.*
> *I, like an usurpt towne, to'another due,*
> *Labour to'admit you, but Oh, to no end,*
> *Reason your viceroy in mee, mee should defend,*
> *But is captiv'd, and proves weake or untrue.*
> *Yet dearely' I love you, 'and would be loved faine,*
> *But am betroth'd unto your enemie:*
> *Divorce mee, 'untie, or breake that knot againe;*
> *Take mee to you, imprison mee, for I*
> *Except you enthrall mee, never shall be free,*
> *Nor ever chast, except you ravish mee.*[8]

part III. truths

8.

sacred sexuality:
an emotional biology

"Emotion always has its roots in the unconscious and manifests itself in the body."
Irene Claremont de Castillejo

*T*ime *Magazine* begins an issue dedicated to human sexuality with this provocative introduction:

> *Of all the splendidly ridiculous, transcendently fulfilling things humans do, it's sex—with its countless permutations of practices and partners—that most confounds understanding. What in the world are we doing? Why in the world are we so consumed by it? The impulse to procreate may lie at the heart of sex, but like the impulse to nourish ourselves, it is merely the starting point for an astonishingly varied banquet. Bursting from our sexual center is a whole spangle of other things—art, song, romance, obsession, rapture, sorrow, companionship, love, even violence and criminality—all playing an enormous role in everything from our physical health to our emotional health to our politics, our communities, our very life spans.*

> *Why should this be so? Did nature simply overload us in the mating department, hot-wiring us for the sex that is so central to the survival of the species, and never mind the sometimes sloppy consequences? Or is there something smarter and subtler at work, some larger interplay among sexuality, life and what it means to be human?* (Time, Jan.19, 2004, p. 64)

Yes, I believe there *is* something "smarter and more subtle at work." But for many of us, our view of sexuality has been so legislated and permeated by religious lies, particularly a division between body and soul, we can't seem to reconcile our biological and spiritual needs, much less understand a theology of sexuality. We can't understand that in order to enjoy the *wholeness* of our emotional, relational, and erotic beings—our sacred sexuality—we need simply to accept the unconditional freedom of God's original plan. As we take a close look at the biological, spiritual, and theological aspects of this plan, we begin to realize that in a kingdom where grace is the currency, there is no room for a language of control.

The wonderful truth of this plan reveals that when we accept and enjoy what is true and beautiful—we are *free*. Free to give love, not spend lust. Free to share ourselves, not possess others. We are free to caress our lover, not "cop a feel." Free to view the human body (clothed or unclothed) in wonder, not voyeuristic shame. We are free to understand God is *for* our enjoyment of sexuality, not *against* our deepest erotic desires. He is enthusiastically *for* all that we are as whole beings as we enjoy the freedom and communion of both soul *and* body.

When we enjoy the freedom language of grace and do not languish behind prison bars of religious control, we begin to understand God's intention for our life. In fact, we realize the *very meaning of life*. This essence of existence is joyfully proclaimed again and again in Holy Scripture:

You don't believe God loves you?

"For God so loved the world that he gave his only son" (John 3:16).

You don't believe that God is a gift to you?

He said, "This is my body given for you" (Luke 22:19).

You think God wants to keep you from enjoying life to the fullest?

"He came so you can have real and eternal life, more and better life than you ever dreamed of" (John 10:10).

You think God is a tyrant, a slave-driver?

On the contrary, "He came to himself take the form of a slave" (Phil. 2:7).

You think God will spank and condemn you if He gets the chance?

He says, "By believing in me, anyone can have a whole and lasting life. I didn't go to all the trouble of sending my Son merely to point an accusing finger, telling you how bad you are. I came to help, to put you right again. Anyone who trusts in me is set free" (John 3:17).

You think God means for us to live a boring life?

He says, "Take your everyday, ordinary life—your sleeping, eating, going-to-work, and walking-around life—and place it before me as an offering. Embracing what I have accomplished for you is the best thing you can do for me.

Unlike the culture around you, always dragging you down to its level of immaturity, I want to bring out the best in you" (Romans 12:1).

You think God means for us to live a sexless life?

He says, "Husbands, go all out in your love for your wives, exactly as I did for the church—a love marked by giving, not getting...And this is why a man leaves father and mother and cherishes his wife. No longer two, they become 'one flesh'" (Eph. 5:25-33).

You think God doesn't understand our desires?

He says, "Take delight in me, and I will give you your heart's desires" (Psalm 37:4).

Scripture reveals a God who understands our deepest emotional and erotic desires, a God who passionately loves us and calls all our senses to come alive in Him. It emotionally describes a God who longs to woo and romance us, experience mutual interaction and intimacy, and ultimately enjoy sacred consummation in an eternal marriage with Him.

Understanding sacred sexuality requires a look at three remarkable aspects of sex. These aspects in context— biological, spiritual, and theological—embody the very essence of our existence. They show us the liberating truth that *human longings lead to God.* And as we begin to realize that sexuality expresses our spirituality, the hope of knowing an "unknowable" God, seeing an "unseeable" God, and even touching an "untouchable God" seems finally and irrevocably within our grasp.

The Birds and the Bees

Sex, as differentiated in the reproductive functions, simply means male or female. A further nuance is the instinct or attraction drawing one sex toward another, or its manifestation in life and conduct through the sexual act. Biology means the science of life or living matter in all its forms, especially in regards to origin, growth, reproduction, structure, and behavior.

In biology, sexuality encompasses the reproductive mechanism as well as the basic biological drive and includes sexual intercourse and sexual contact in all its forms. There are emotional, relational, and erotic aspects of sexuality. These relate to the bond that exists between people, which may be expressed through the profound feelings and emotions of a sexual act.

Most of us can instantly recall our first love. Singer and Songwriter Tim McGraw describes it this way: "I worked so hard for that first kiss, and a heart don't forget something like that. Like an old photograph, time can make a feeling fade. But the memory of a first love never fades away." In fact, Albert Einstein asks this question: "How on earth are you ever going to explain in terms of chemistry and physics so important a biological phenomenon as first love?" This initial encounter with love can perhaps be best summed up in the word *attraction.*

Some of us may remember when we began to experience *sexual pleasure.* One of my friends, while giving his young son a bath, went away to get a towel and as he returned, noticed him stroking his penis. Instead of overreacting in shock and with a negative command, he simply said, "Feels good, doesn't it son?" Not all parents would have reacted this way but the functional affirmation of sexual pleasure expressed by this parent bodes well for an open, healthy and positive discussion of the beauty of sexual pleasure at the appropriate time.

Some of us also remember the fateful day in our childhood when we heard the answer to the innocent question, "*Mom, where do babies come from?*" But unfortunately, more of us than not had parents who felt the best way to answer that question was to evade it. And so what should have been a safe and natural time and place to understand the beauty of bringing another human being into existence instead became an "adult magazine," a person of the opposite sex, a dysfunctional adult, or myriad other unintended ways.

Please understand I am not trying to condemn parents with guilt. Many of our parents were children having children and had no parental or religious training about sex themselves. Maybe that's why the Pontifical Council says, "Among the many difficulties parents encounter today...one certainly stands out: giving children an adequate preparation for adult life, particularly with regard to education in the true meaning of sexuality."[1]

Let's examine more closely three emotional aspects of biological sexuality. Attraction, pleasure, and procreation, while not an exhaustive list, do provide a starting place in educating our children (and possibly even ourselves) about the birds and the bees.

Attraction

Attraction, for our purposes, means "a person that draws, attracts, allures, or entices." We call sexual attraction many things: charm, charisma, chemistry, glamour, enchantment, first love, sex appeal, animal magnetism, drawing power, seductiveness, sexiness, "the go from down under," and the "it" factor, to name only a few. Countless authors have written books about it from the *Law of Attraction* and *Rules of Attraction*, to *Dangers of Attraction* and *Fatal Attraction*.

Attraction is associated with the part of the brain known as the hypothalamus that produces different reactions in the body such as sexual arousal, increased heart rate, and perspiration. It also produces oxytocin, which helps increase the level of one's trust in other people and further enhances bonding between lovers.

And although everyone has certain specific preferences as to what they find attractive in another individual, there are a number of qualities we nearly all find attractive. Men tend to prefer women with features that suggest youth and fertility, including a low waist-to-hip ratio, full lips and soft facial features. Recent studies confirm that women have strong preferences for virile male beauty—taut bodies, broad shoulders, clear skin and defined, masculine facial features, all of which may indicate sexual potency and good genes. We also know that women are attracted to men who look as if they have wealth or the ability to acquire it, and that men and women strongly value intelligence in a mate. Preferences for these qualities—beauty, brains, and resources—are universal. George Clooney and Beyoncé are sex symbols for predictable emotional and biological reasons.

So what about the less obvious clues of attraction? Attraction has long been described as a process of enchantment, but scientists have found that there may be more truth to this than meets the eye. Research by biologists Astrid Juette and Professor Karl Grammer from the University of Vienna has found that a man's perception of a woman's attractiveness is altered by the chemical signals she sends out.[2]

Each of us are thought to have our own distinctive scent, much like a signature or fingerprint. While not fully understood, we do know that smell is an important clue. People appear to literally sniff out their mates. In studies, people tend to rate the scent of T-shirts worn by others with dissimilar smells as most attractive. Female pheromones may trick men into believing a woman looks more attractive than she is. Pheromones are odorless chemical signals, which affect behavior. Juette and Grammer's research has shown that humans have sex-appeal pheromones that work on a subtle subconscious level.

It seems that human female pheromones have an especially cunning role in persuading a man to find a woman attractive. They appear to block a man's ability to judge a woman's attractiveness by the way she looks and the sound of her voice. The subtle scent signal acts as a love potion, turning the man's head even though on the basis of sight and sound alone, he might not be interested.

The biologists exposed a group of young men unknowingly to synthetic vaginal pheromones. Their reactions to photographs of women and female voices were compared with what happened when the pheromones were replaced with ordinary water. They found that pheromones had the effect of increasing the attractiveness ratings the men gave the women.

The amount of testosterone in the men's saliva increased after they had inhaled the pheromones. Merely by smelling the pheromones, the men's ability to process information from their eyes and ears was altered.

The scientists concluded that "'primary affective reactions' as induced by smell, may alter the processing of visual and auditive stimuli." This could be what sexual "chemistry" is all about. To this day, when I get even a faint smell of "Sweet Honesty" perfume, I think of my first crush, Marilyn. I am transported back to a time and place that was over three decades ago—as if it were yesterday.

So we can deduce that attraction is determined by a mix of biological and emotional factors, some of which we are aware of consciously, and some of which we experience indirectly.

Could this "law of attraction" be part of the original plan of creation? And could it be that we do not gain full awareness of our own body until we see (and perhaps smell) the body of another? In this awareness could we sense a call to join our body and soul to another in order to be fully complete?

Attraction has been a mysterious phenomenon throughout history. No matter the physical differences and religious beliefs of myriad societies, somehow most of us continue to get together with a mate who brings us pleasure.

Pleasure

We are hot-wired for pleasure. In essence, we all crave sensual activities that cause enjoyment. The following description of pleasure comes from C.S. Lewis's book *Screwtape Letters* which contains musings of a fictional elder demon teaching a younger, less experienced demon:

> *"Never forget that when we are dealing with any pleasure in its healthy and normal and satisfying form, we are, in a sense, on the Enemy's ground. I know we have won many a soul through pleasure. All the same, it is His invention, not ours. He made the pleasures: all our research so far has not enabled us to produce one. All we can do is to encourage humans to take the pleasures which our Enemy has produced, at times, or in ways, or in degrees, which He has forbidden. Hence we always try to work away from the natural condition of any pleasure to that in which it is least natural, least redolent of its Maker, and least pleasurable. An ever-increasing craving for an ever diminishing pleasure is the formula....To get the man's soul and give nothing in return—that is what really gladdens our Father's heart."*[3]

For most people, the orgasm is the benchmark of pleasure. The fact that it produces the most enjoyable sensations and the strongest desires that we are likely to ever experience suggests that sexual activity is effectively one of the most important and pleasurable things we do in life.

Thankfully, centuries of religious lies have failed to turn the pleasure of sexual activity into something merely functional and boring. Typical heterosexual couples make love an average of a hundred times a year. Assuming they keep up this pace, they will end up having sex as many as four thousand times.[4]

In addition to sex with a partner, many people also seek sexual pleasure alone. Men typically learn to masturbate in adolescence and some studies say they keep it up daily until their twenties and go on to masturbate an average of five thousand times in fifty to sixty years.[5] Altogether, the average man can expect to experience over nine thousand orgasms during the course of his life. And bear in mind these studies were conducted before erectile stimulants such as Viagra came into prominence.

Other studies say that women begin masturbating at a similar age but with half the frequency as men. They typically enjoy sexual stimulation, either alone or with a partner, for a lifetime total of five to six thousand times.

It should come as no surprise that sexual pleasure consumes an inordinate amount of our thinking. The typical male thinks about sex at least once, if not a few times a day and the typical female a few times per week.[6] Mignon McLaughlin jokingly said, "A nymphomaniac is a woman as obsessed with sex as the average man." But the truth is that sexual energy for both male and female is a life force that is with us from birth.

The first instruction to Adam & Eve was to be "fruitful and multiply," or in other words, "go and start making babies." And we know how God biologically designed babies to be made. The Bible uses the Hebrew word Yada or "to know intimately" when Adam and Eve came together to reproduce. Sexual pleasure is one of God's wonderful rewards to us for continuing to make babies.

Procreation

This unusual word means simply to produce offspring—to make babies. And you can't typically make babies without sexual activity. Playwrights have had a field day with the

biological miracle. Shakespeare cryptically says it this
way: "He plough'd her, and she cropp'd." And the Austrian
playwright Ludwig Wittgenstein says more philosophically,
"It is so characteristic, that just when the mechanics of
reproduction are so vastly improved, there are fewer and
fewer people who know how the music should be played."

The term procreation seems to be popping up in
contemporary society more often these days. Creative minds
in the travel industry have labeled the newest vacation craze,
the "Procreation Vacation." On one website, the marketing
copy reads "not as reclusive as the honeymoon and not as
crowded as the 'babymoon,' the procreation vacation is
somewhere in between."⁷ By the way, a babymoon is a vacation
taken while pregnant or, sometimes, for new parents. The
idea is to let the soon-to-be parents be pampered, live it up
(minus the alcohol) and, in general, enjoy the last moment
of peace, quiet and adults-only entertainment of their lives.

The procreation vacation focuses on the couple hoping
to conceive. Hotels and resorts are offering romantic
vacation packages complete with all the details, doctors, and
amenities needed to make this vacation unforgettable.

Of course, procreation plays an important part in
literature, too. It is intriguing to note that Shakespeare's
sonnets 1–37 were called Procreation Sonnets. They are so
named because they reason that the young man, to whom
they are addressed, should marry and father children, hence,
procreate. Throughout the sonnets, Shakespeare makes the
case that the child will be a copy of the young man, and he
will therefore create a legacy.

In the Bible, God's first admonition to man was to
make children. "Be fruitful and increase in number; and
fill the earth" (Gen. 1:28). The Hebrew Bible also exclaims,
"Blessed is the man whose quiver is full [of children],"⁸ and
"Children are a reward from the Lord."⁹ We realize through
scripture that we were innately wired from the beginning of
time to procreate.

But why *do* we have children? They cost too much money. In fact, it doesn't make economic sense at all to have a child. Sources estimate the financial liability of raising a child (including college) ranges from $700,000 to a stunning $1.5 million per child. Children also cost too much of ourselves. They first steal our hearts, then break them, and sometimes even trample them. And we let them. We bring these tiny little strangers into our home and decide to love them with abandon, for as long as we live, despite the consequences.

We realize that the purpose in procreation is not merely to reproduce and fill the earth; it also fulfills the very meaning of our being and existence. Leaving behind a legacy on earth is one of man's deepest innate desires and children embody the quintessential fulfillment of this need. Children also provide a profound happiness and completion, and represent tangible symbols of creation and the Trinity.

Just as God the Father, Son, and Holy Spirit created us and "shares in common" with each other and with us, we then also create and share communion with each other *and with the Trinity* through our sexuality and procreation. So then, in a divine and mysterious way, "sexual love becomes an earthly representation in some sense of the inner life of the Trinity and the union of God with humanity."[10] Each time we see a father, mother, and child, we see in essence a representation of the Trinity. In this way, parents, by considering the mysterious bond of love with our children, discover a symbol for the eternal and selfless love God has for mankind. We find in our sexuality and procreation a transcendent way to make the invisible *divine mystery* visible.

Sacred sexuality through the wonder and beauty of procreation provides an opportunity to create an earthly representation of a divine mystery. The *Catechism* says, "God has revealed his innermost secret: God himself is an eternal exchange of love, Father, Son, and Holy Spirit, and he has destined us to share in that exchange"[11] (n.221). Pope John Paul II states it this way: "God is an eternal

Communion of Persons." The term communion is derived from Latin *communio*, which means "sharing in common."[12] For some unknown reason, God has decided to create and share in communion with mankind.

As we examine the emotional biology of procreation, it becomes easier to empathize with the deep pain experienced by infertile couples who desire children. It also helps to understand why homosexual couples fight for the right to have children. Our innate desires are wrapped up in God's original plan to "be fruitful and increase our number, and fill the earth."

Biological Communion

An emotional biology helps us see that attraction, pleasure, and procreation provide a crucial foundation for an understanding of sacred sexuality. Although each aspect is biological and scientific, it also contains deep emotional considerations. Sacred sexuality is both physical *and* emotional. It is a beautiful combination of biological copulation with an attractive person while experiencing passionate pleasure. But, it is much more than just copulation and pleasure.

In true communion, we are not just "having sex," we are "making love." In fact, the way we interact is as much about "making love" as the actual act of intercourse. However, when the interaction of spiritual relationship is absent, "making love" quickly degenerates into merely "having sex."

Sexuality that celebrates a sacred essence consists of a deep cherishing exchange of love by two people in the emotional, spiritual, and theological dimensions of their beings. As we look at the second aspect of sacred sexuality, relational spirituality, we begin to understand that making love is a way of life and that every day can be foreplay.

9.

sacred sexuality:
a relational spirituality

"Don't have sex, man. It leads to kissing and pretty soon you have to start talking to them."
Steve Martin

Sex begins in the kitchen and you don't have to be a good cook to find it there. Simply gather a handful of the succulent fruit described in this chapter and your mate will be literally eating out of your hand while racing you to the bedroom for an endless time of wild and abandoned lovemaking.

Does this sound too good to be true? It's not. This is what can happen when you enjoy the freedom of unconditional sexuality. Making love becomes a way of life. It is the spiritual essence of each day. And in this sense every day is foreplay. The soft brush of a fleeting kiss as you awaken, a brief time of thoughtful conversation over a cup of coffee, a warm and close embrace at hello and goodbye, showing affection to unruly children, expressing exuberance about life, practicing serenity in turbulent times, and displaying a sense of compassion to others, are all as much "making love" as when actual sexual intercourse takes place.

If you have any experience with the Bible, these words should sound hauntingly familiar. The previous paragraph is simply a paraphrase of Galatians 5, which describes the character qualities of what is called "the fruit of the Spirit." The thought-provoking and controversial words contained therein provide the spiritual essence for this aspect of sacred sexuality.

The Fruit of the Spirit

Galatians teaches that good fruit characterizes a satisfying *relationship with the Spirit*. This list of moral qualities or "fruits" produced by following the Spirit leads to freedom and communion with God. Religion worries that "living by the Spirit" instead of rules leads to immorality and sin. Just the opposite will be the case. A relationship with the Spirit produces the moral qualities that epitomize a life of unconditional sexuality.

The scripture again reiterates that we have been called to a free life, though it states that we should guard against using this freedom as an excuse to do anything we want. This type of living eventually destroys our freedom. Rather, we are to use our freedom to serve one another in love. Everything we know about God can be summed up in a single sentence: *Love others as you love yourself.* That's true freedom. If we take each other for granted, watch out—in no time at all, our love for each other will be annihilated.

We should instead live freely, animated and motivated by the Spirit. Then we won't feed the compulsions of selfishness. There is a root of self-interest in all of us that is at odds with a free spirit, just as the free spirit is incompatible with selfishness. We are not to live by how we feel—that's not the freedom that scripture talks about. We instead must choose to live by the Spirit and so escape the schizophrenia of a control-oriented existence.

A *reliance* upon the Spirit will enable us to move beyond feelings to freedom. At the moment of salvation, the Holy Spirit takes up residence in the life of a believer and becomes the source of power for his life. The theme of Galatians 5 is the Spirit-controlled life and what it produces—the fruit of the Spirit: "love, joy, peace, long-suffering, gentleness, goodness, faith, meekness, [and] self control" (vv. 22-23).

The basis of a fruitful Christian life lived to the glory of is the power of the Holy Spirit.

When we try to get our own way all the time, it results in repetitive, loveless and unfulfilling sex; mental and emotional garbage; frenzied and joyless grabs for happiness; paranoid loneliness; all-consuming-yet-never-satisfied wants; a brutal temper; an impotence to love or be loved; divided homes and divided lives; the vicious habit of depersonalizing everyone; and uncontrolled and uncontrollable addiction. We must not use our freedom in this way.

But when we live out a spiritual life in freedom, God brings gifts into our lives, much the same way that fruit appears in an orchard. These fruits of the Spirit are the underlying spirit of sacred sexuality.

Love

Love takes first place. We are to love our mate unconditionally just as Christ loves the church. From the second Vatican Council of the Catholic Church we read, "Man can fully discover his true self only in a sincere giving of himself."[1] Self-realization only comes from loving each other as God loves. C.S. Lewis writes, "To love at all is to be vulnerable. Love anything, and your heart will certainly be wrung and possibly broken. If you want to make sure of keeping it intact, you must give your heart to no one. Wrap it carefully round with hobbies and little luxuries; avoid all entanglements; lock it up safe in the casket or coffin of your selfishness. But in that casket—safe, dark, motionless, airless—it will change. It will not be broken; it will become unbreakable, impenetrable, irredeemable."[2]

Love by its very nature must be a reciprocal gift and is beautifully symbolized by the unending circle of the wedding ring, which represents God's eternal love for us *and* our love for each other. "God inscribed the call to divine love in our bodies—in our sexuality—right from the beginning."[3]

That is why the following scripture is called the greatest commandment and encompasses the very meaning of life. "Love one another as I have loved you."[4] All the other fruits in the following list *define and flow from love.* In the words of the inimitable Beatles, "All you need is love."

Joy

Joy results from a healthy relationship with God. When our spiritual relationship falls apart because of broken commitments on our part, there is a loss of joy. When there is conflict and bitterness in our relationship, there is no joy. In the Bible, the fruit of the Spirit that King David missed more than any other was joy. When he was separated in his relationship with God because of his sin, he cried in repentance, "Restore to me the joy of my salvation."[5]

I will never forget hearing a story recounted at a marriage seminar when I was an impressionable young married man. Our teachers (Bob and Rosemary) were a couple from Ft. Lauderdale, Fl. and were obviously happily married. They told about a date night when the kids were safely away at a babysitter and they were trying to decide what to do.

Suddenly Rosemary mischievously began to strip off her clothes and revealed lacy and completely sheer lingerie underneath. She then laughingly told Bob to take his clothes off and go to the garage and get into their old Volkswagen Beetle convertible. The garage door opened and they proceeded into the darkness, naked and bound for a starry ride along the beach on a perfect Florida night.

As luck would have it, as they were reveling and "enjoying" the sexy ride, the VW sputtered to a halt and died. With nothing but a birthday suit and a completely sheer negligee between them, they were awkwardly stranded on an isolated road along the beach. Instead of getting tense, they decided to make the best of it. They took the opportunity to enjoy something they had never tried as married adults.

Since the car was already parked, they began to make love in the cramped quarters of the backseat. Sure enough an hour or so later, a flashlight shone in and a policeman asked them to explain themselves.

I will never forget the obvious (albeit embarrassed) joy the couple had in recounting that story to our small group of young married couples. My wife and I looked at each other with a grin of anticipation, and a small part of the religious legalism we had grown up with melted away. We realized that it was possible to actually enjoy our sexuality.

Please understand, I'm not talking about taking a sexual fantasy such as exhibitionism and making it real life, but I am talking about lightening up our prudish ways of thinking and enjoying the freedom of our sexuality. We need to enjoy the story of life because life is not a dress rehearsal and the play is too short. Joy goes beyond happiness. Happiness depends on earthly circumstances, but joy is the spiritual belief that the end of the story has already been written. As Christians, no matter how dark this story called life gets at times, we know that it climaxes happily ever after in eternity.

As Christians, we can experience joy without happiness. Writer Anne Lamott, who has chronicled a personal life fraught with difficulty and suffering says it this way: "Joy is the best makeup." When the makeup of life is washed away by the tears of suffering or difficulties, our countenance still somehow displays the inner beauty of the joy of the Lord.

Peace

When erotic play and sexual union are genuine and truly rewarding for a couple, all of the big problems in life seem like little ones. They experience a life of Shalom. Shalom is the word in Hebrew for total peace. It represents full and total peace in the emotional, relational, and sensual aspects of our lives. It is a gift from God for every one of us to accept and enjoy all of life.

When we collapse onto the bed after a beautiful time of "making love" with our mate, we sense an "all is right in the world" feeling. No matter our financial, family, or even global problems, for a brief time, we experience Shalom—a full and total peace.

After your next sexual adventure, take a few moments and press into the feelings you have during that spiritual time of contemplation and gratefully accept the peace you feel. Take a few moments and verbally express the depths of what you feel to your mate as you lay together.

Patience

Patience is the opposite of "fits of rage" or short temper. It is the quality of seeking to understand our mate even when wronged or irritated by them. It is restraining our emotion when exhausted by work and stress. Patience flows from an awareness of love and is willing to stick it out though thick or thin, good or bad, in sickness and in health.

Practically speaking, patience gives us the ability to appreciate and nurture our lover. It is an exercise of "suffering long" with each other. For example, sex therapist Betty Tyndall says that one in four young girls have been introduced to sex in a less than healthy way. A patient lover realizes the need to communicate and proceed slowly when "monsters from the past" climb into bed and inhibit a time of healthy sexuality. Patience encourages open communication, which in turn gradually provides the hope of freedom from the guilt of the past. True love suffers long and is kind.

Kindness and Goodness

These two fruits when joined with patience result in a gracious disposition, no matter the provocation. They represent a sense of compassion in the heart, and a belief that a basic holiness permeates all people. If a person possesses both kindness and goodness, the magic in his or her life has somehow not been eradicated and replaced by cynicism. For example, they would forgo an orgasm to make sure their mate experiences one.

And on the other hand, kindness grants permission during the hectic times of everyday life to say it's okay to have a "quickie." A supreme act of kindness and goodness for both lovers can be to acknowledge the need for sex that is fast, provides a release of sexual energy for a man and a confirmation of oneness for a woman.

Faithfulness

This is the quality of keeping commitments in relationships. True faithfulness is not blind loyalty, but understands when to extend devotion and trust. A faithful person is steady in allegiance and affection. The ideal of faithfulness implies steadfast adherence to a person to which one is bound by an oath or obligation. A faithful person does not sleep around nor give their betrothed heart away—especially to someone who has not pledged or earned their trust.

It is still hard for me to comprehend that Chris and I have been married over thirty years. At times, it feels as though the two of us are giddy eighteen year olds in the middle of some sort of time traveling dream. It seems that we blinked and were suddenly an older married couple.

In talking to couples who have been married fifty, sixty and even seventy years, the distinguishing fruit of their lives is faithfulness. These couples have explained to me that faithfulness is not perfection. It is commitment through hard times and good times. They have recounted times of betrayal and heartache, yet the fruit of faithfulness enabled them to somehow stay together.

One eighty-plus year old married man in a laughing but serious way told me that when you can't physically have sex without Viagra, faithfulness becomes a huge quality. As an almost imperceptible tear came to his eye, he talked about walking through infidelities on both their parts, and despite the horrific mistakes, eventually realizing the significance of the marriage covenant they had struck together.

Gentleness

This fruit is the opposite of selfishness. Gentle people are not arrogant, malicious, and jealous of each other. Gentleness is an expression of humility, considering the needs and hurts of others before one's personal desires. A gentle answer to your mate will diffuse their anger. A person who practices spiritual gentleness does not need to force their way through life, rather they tend to yield control and practice yielding to grace.

At times, a gentle touch during lovemaking can be more powerful than the most intense orgasm. Inevitably, after a few days, the memory of the orgasm is long since forgotten, but the remembrance of a gentle touch lingers. In our culture, gentleness is a lost art. Many men feel that gentleness is a sign of weakness. But on the contrary, Chinese writer Han Suyin says, "There is nothing stronger in the world than gentleness."

Self-Control

This discipline is the opposite of self-indulgence. People who practice self-control do not use other people to gratify their own appetites. Nor do they allow others to use them. They have the strength to say no to themselves, and are able to marshal and direct their energies wisely.

We tend to trade the ultimate for the immediate. It strikes me as important that many definitions of self-control describe it as the capacity to efficiently manage the future. Many things affect one's ability to exert self-control, but self-control particularly requires sufficient glucose levels in the brain.[6]

Many people I have talked with over the course of thirty years in the ministry have experienced moral breakdowns that have affected the course of their lives forever. It is important to understand the propensity for a lack of self-control during times of significant life change. A simple but effective adage is that of the acrostic HALT. Recognize that when you are *h*ungry, *a*ngry, *l*onely and *t*ired, special care must be taken to exert self-control in all areas of life—but especially in the area of our sexuality.

A Life of Freedom

This list of qualities paints a picture of relational sexuality that is built and nourished by the presence of the Spirit. Religious rules and regulations are helpless in bringing this about; they only get in the way. For those of us who belong to Christ and really care about our lover, everything connected with getting our own way and mindlessly responding to what Western Civilization calls necessities is killed off for good—dead.

When we choose to relate to our lover through the Spirit, let's make sure that we do not just hold it as an ideal in our bodies or a sentiment in our souls, but rather work out its implications in every detail, in each day of our lives. That means we will not compare ourselves with our lover as if one of us were better and the other worse. We have far more sensual things to do with our lives. Each of us is an original sacred and sexual being created by God the Father, wooed by Christ the Bridegroom, and given life by the Holy Spirit.

As we develop the fruits of the spirit in our lives, the controls and legalism of religion lose their grip on our body and soul. We come to see and experience our sexuality as a multi-sensual theology that provides a way to clearly experience "the divine mystery" of God while living daily through the power of the Incarnation. And we can do all this while celebrating the intimacy and freedom of a sacramental life. If that seems exciting, read on.

10.

sacred sexuality:
a theology of the body

"The body, and the body alone, is capable of making visible what is invisible: the spiritual and divine."
Pope John Paul II

By now we understand that sex is not just about sex. It provides a way to understand God. Where religion makes simple ideas about God complex, sex can make complex ideas about God simple. The way we live out our sexuality expresses who we are, who God is, what love is, how we relate to others, and why we are here. It is the essence of existence.

However, many people are uncomfortable with an emphasis on sex when it comes to theology (a study of God). As we understand the context of the previous two chapters, we begin to realize that as sexual beings, "in a certain sense, the only way we can experience the spiritual world is in and through the physical world and in and through our bodies."[1]

By taking on a body through the Incarnation, the revered St. Athanasius who penned the definitive Christian classic regarding the Incarnation said, "God chose to humbly 'meet us where we look for Him most, and that is in our sensuality.'"[2] Unfortunately, religious lies have led us to think that our bodies, and especially our sexuality, are hindrances to the spiritual life. In a recent online survey in which 98% of respondents considered themselves spiritual,

8 out of 10 believe that the soul is better than the body. This thinking could not be further from the truth.

The false teaching of heresy says the body is bad, but the true teaching of theology says the "body is so good you can't even fathom it."3 The problem with religious lies is that they have failed to help us see that the body and sex are pathways to an intimate knowledge of God. An erotic theology affirms that our sexuality is sacred and that we most intimately encounter God through the sensuality of our bodies. Indeed, "the body itself is in some sense a sacrament."4

If the Bible were a movie, it would be rated NC-17. It is an erotic book that does not shy away from the fleshly and sometimes messy aspects of our sexuality. But many religions have literally torn the sensual pages with which they disagree from the Bible. For instance, many conservative churches have deleted the wild dancing of David in the Old Testament and removed the first miracle of Jesus when He created wine to celebrate a sexual consummation. Despite historical fact, they insist Jesus created grape juice. Chances are you have never attended a religious service that celebrated the eroticism of the Old Testament or explained the difference between art and pornography. And I wonder if your religious teaching has helped you understand the pleasure of masturbation or the healthy way to enjoy sexual fantasy with your mate.

I recently conducted a gathering where leaders, ministers, and theologians from the Eastern Orthodox, Catholic, Anglican, and Evangelical traditions discussed marriage and sexuality. As orthodox beliefs, theologies, and writings essential to each faith were discussed, it became increasingly obvious that the Evangelical tradition (of which I am a part) has absolutely no theology of the body. As my pastor and I listened to the animated and intelligent discussion of other faiths, we realized the crucial need for a better understanding of orthodoxy. By orthodoxy I mean, a general knowledge of *accepted and established faith traditions*. As the old adage goes, those of us without an adequate knowledge of history will be doomed to repeat the mistakes of those who have gone before us.

Theology of the Body

As we wind our way through the maze of religious teachings (both true and false) it is important to know and understand orthodox beliefs concerning sexuality. Orthodox beliefs are accepted and established faith traditions that have survived the test of time. I am not talking about a denomination here, but rather a set of beliefs that have been agreed upon and tested against scripture historically by church leaders.

"The orthodox position concerning sexuality has been gloriously—dare I say *definitively*—explained and defended by Pope John Paul II in his magisterial *The Theology of the Body*. Based on a series of weekly general audiences delivered between 1979 and 1984, *The Theology of the Body* is essential reading not only for traditional Catholics but for Evangelical Protestants as well."[5]

Because this work is so profound, we will use *The Theology of the Body* as the definitive foundation for this chapter and will employ the three aspects of rhetoric (the art of persuading through language) to provide a structure. I believe that persuasion comes most effectively from the basis of freedom and not from force or control. Let's quickly review the three aspects of rhetoric.

First, I can persuade you if you believe me credible (ethos). This kind of persuasion can be achieved by what I say. Second, persuasion can come through you, the reader, when the words stir your emotions (pathos). For instance, we learn better when we are happy—or sad. Third, persuasion happens when I prove a truth by means of a persuasive argument (logos).

Let's begin by examining the defining statement of John Paul II's *The Theology of the Body*. It reads, "The body, and the body alone, is capable of making visible what is invisible: the spiritual and divine. It was created to transfer into the visible reality of the world, the mystery hidden since time immemorial in God, and thus to be a sign of it" (Feb. 20, 1980). Christopher West explains further, "Somehow the body enables us to 'see' spiritual realities, even the eternal mystery 'hidden' in God."[6] This sounds wonderful but how is it so?

As we have seen previously, human nature is both soul and body. Orthodox teaching has always maintained that although we do not share Jesus' unique God-Man status, we do share something of His incarnational nature: We are not souls trapped in bodies or bodies covering souls, but "enfleshed" souls—both fully spiritual and fully physical.

It's from this dimension that Pope John Paul II studies the body in a startling new way—not as biological matter, but as a *theology*, a study of God. We know that the body isn't divine, but as this epic study explains, it can point us to the divine mystery. John Paul II says, "Through the fact that the Word of God became flesh, the body entered theology... through the main door."[7]

The Logos of the Father (Creation)

In order to understand a theology of the body, we must go back to God's original plan before sin distorted everything. The original experiences of the body and sexuality offer what John Paul II calls an "echo" of the beginning.

In John 1 we are at the inception of a story that reveals to us the most profound mysteries of life. This story is about God and His *desire to share* or "make love" with His creation. These verses provide a sort of beginning to the beginning. Chronologically, the story begins in eternity and then moves to creation.

The opening of the book of John echoes Genesis, but where Genesis refers only to God the Father's activity at the beginning of creation, in John we learn of two other members of the Godhead—God the Son, and God the Holy Spirit—who also existed before creation occurred.

To fully understand whom the Word is, we must start before the beginning; in fact, John says we must begin "before the world began" with the relationship shared between the Father, the Son and the Holy Spirit. This mutual and mysterious relationship provides a key to understanding the first concept of creation—that of original solitude.

Original Solitude

First, we should examine the aspect of solitude in God's original plan. "God said, 'It is not good for man to be alone.'"[8] Obviously, this solitude represents man alone without woman. But there is more. As Adam names the animals and lives alone among them, he begins to realize that he is different. He understands that he is a *person with freedom*, and as a free person he can choose what to do with his body and what he thinks will bring him happiness. He understands that this ability to choose makes him completely different than all the animals that surround him in the garden. Despite modern propaganda and the pressure of the media to make animals far more than they are, we know intuitively that animals simply aren't people. They do not possess personhood. No other creature on earth but man has the extraordinary *freedom and ability to choose.*

Why did God endow Adam with freedom? The Bible says the divine reason for original creation was to invite man to exchange love. And true love cannot be forced. Unlike the animals, Adam realizes that he is the only creature that has the ability to say "Yes" or "No" to God's love. He also realizes that he has been invited to "make love" with the God of creation and that knowledge compounds his feelings of loneliness. At this point in time, Adam represents all of us, and his erotic longings tell him there must be more to life. He realizes he is the only creature who is a person.

Because he has been created in the image of God, and since the intercourse of love between the Trinity (Father, Son and Holy Spirit) existed before the world began, he experiences a bodily desire to make "God-like" love with someone like himself. That's why God responds, "It is not good for man to be alone."⁹

God's solution for this erotic hunger to love and be loved is taken not from the earth, but from within Adam's body. This provision of another person created from Adam's personhood (his soul and body) foreshadows profound implications. Through this multi-layered act of creation, God provides man an extraordinary and tangible way to "make love" to Him. This woman, so much like man and yet so different, gives man a sacramental opportunity to "love as God loves." Through our bodies, we find a God not outside of ourselves, but one who longs for an internal and eternal exchange (a communion) of love and unity.

Original Unity

We do not read of Adam's excitement about any of the animals. But when he saw (and probably smelled) this attractive new person walking through the garden, he got really excited. In fact, he composed the first poem on earth when he exclaimed upon seeing Eve, "This at last is bone of my bone, and flesh of my flesh!"¹⁰ The full meaning of his words are hard to grasp in English. But if I could take liberties here and translate for him, I believe that in Hebrew he was saying in breathless wonder and awe, "Oh God, she is hot!"

The words of this poem help us understand the intense erotic attraction Adam felt for her. First, it's important to note that it was her body that immediately fascinates Adam. The body of this woman expresses a human persona, and that personhood combined with her body makes her appear much different from the animals. Adam realizes that she emerged literally from his flesh and from his bones.

The original man and woman have much in common. They are both made in God's image, both have bodies, both different from the animals, and both invited to a mysterious and divine love.

Genesis 2:24 says, "Therefore a man leaves his father and mother and cleaves to his wife, and they become one flesh." Adam realizes in Eve not just a biological mate (even the animals mate in a biological sense) but also a spiritual and *theological* mate.

Even though theologians traditionally have said we image God as individuals (and we certainly do), John Paul II takes it further when he says that man becomes the image of God not so much in the moment of solitude as in the moment of communion.[11]

It is important to note here that moments of communion such as this can also be experienced by single adults. The ultimate fulfillment of solitude comes only from a sacred union or consummation with God. Christopher West in his book *Good News About Sex & Marriage* makes a powerful point when he says that singleness does not cause sexual disorder. Sin causes sexual disorder. Marriage does not remedy sexual disorder. God does. Single and married adults alike must experience the redemption of their sexuality in Christ.

It is also important for couples to realize that one cannot depend upon the other to provide ultimate satisfaction for our deepest needs. We can get into deep trouble when we expect our mates to provide what only God can ultimately give. It is only through sacred sexuality that we all can realize an earthly revelation of divine relationship. The theological symbolism of sexual union (whether single or married) makes visible the invisible mystery of God.

Original Nakedness

As a parent, I would have cherished this knowledge of a theology of the body to provide to my children in their formative years. For example, one of my young daughters, as we were walking through the *Louvre* in Paris, exclaimed in disgust, "Daddy, why are all of the people naked?" I made an embarrassed and ultimately futile attempt to explain. But I think I can do a better job now. So, if you have ever wondered why most of the great masterpieces render people naked, read on.

In the creation account, we see that "both man and his wife were naked, and not ashamed."[12] Pope John Paul II makes a huge statement about the importance of this verse. He says that original nakedness is "precisely the key for understanding God's original plan for man." He goes on to say that nakedness without shame "describes their state of consciousness, or even better, their reciprocal experience of the body...with the greatest precision possible."[13]

There was no shame. "Only the nakedness that turns the woman into an 'object' for the man, or vice versa, is a source of shame. The fact that 'they did not feel shame' means that the woman was not an 'object' for the man, nor he for her."[14] Nakedness is a beautiful and natural gift from God when offered in a reciprocal exchange of self-giving. In fact, "'Nakedness' signifies the original good of the divine vision. It signifies the whole simplicity and fullness of this vision, which shows the 'pure' value of man as male and female, the 'pure' value of the body and of sex."[15]

According to St. Augustine, the deepest desire of the human heart is to see another and be seen by that other's loving look.[16] While lust represents a voyeuristic desire to look through a one-way mirror without the effort of self-disclosure, love represents a mutual gaze of desire through a two-way mirror of self-giving and communion. In God's original plan, the sight of a naked body reveals to man a complete reflection of himself and ultimately a holy revelation of God.

In the words of Genesis 1:31, "God saw everything he had made, and it was very good." So why then have we lost sight of God's original plan of nakedness without shame? Why can we not see the spiritual aspects of our humanity and theological aspects of divine mystery that our bodies and sexuality were created to reveal?

Unfortunately, it is the age-old problem of sin. Because God the Father so loved mankind, He gave Adam and Eve the freedom to choose what to do with their bodies. And we all know what happened that fateful day at the Tree. Because of their choice, evil entered into the world and the ability to see with God's eyes was lost. But there is hope. In the words of the song "Amazing Grace," "I once was blind, but now I see."

The German philosopher Max Weber in his *Essays on Sociology* makes a powerful case that since creation, a gradual redemption (what he calls a "redemptive hermeneutic") is taking place on earth.[17] And a pivotal moment of a further redemption of solitude, unity and yes, even nakedness, came when God the Father decided that God the Son would become flesh and dwell on the earth.

The Ethos of the Son (Incarnation)

Ethos refers to the disposition, character, or fundamental values distinctive to a specific person or movement. *The Message* version of John 1:14 describes the ethos of God the Son, Jesus Christ, in this way: "The Word became flesh and blood, and moved into the neighborhood. We saw the glory with our own eyes, the one-of-a-kind glory, like Father, like Son, Generous inside and out, true from start to finish."[18] Jesus knew that in order for our eyes to once again see His "one-of-a-kind" glory, the original element of sight that was lost in sin, He would have to take on a human body.

The ethos of the Incarnation makes possible the seemingly impossible thesis, "to enjoy the freedom of unconditional sexuality." Religion seeks to control us by applying excessive conditions and oppressive rules. But the Incarnation does not give rules to follow; it re-creates in us holy longings and the ability to renew the image of the Creator Father in our bodies. It transforms us by the renewing of our minds in Christ Jesus and to the degree that we accept that transformation, we no longer need conditions and rules, because we no longer desire to break them.

Unconditional freedom is made possible through grace. The only requirement is that we enjoy our freedom.

We are free. We are free to unconditionally enjoy the divine mystery of God's original plan. When we daily accept and enjoy the gift of the Logos of the Father (Creation) combined with the gift of the Ethos of the Son (Incarnation), we begin to understand freedom. We most often refer to grace when we speak about the Incarnation, but Adam and Eve were infused by grace at *Creation*.

However, when they made the choice to disobey God, they "rejected grace." This rejection required a re-creation of original solitude, unity and nakedness that was beautifully "fleshed-out" in the Incarnation. Christ does this in His God-man status by symbolically redeeming original solitude during His time with God in the desert; original unity through performing His first miracle at a celebration of sexual consummation; and original nakedness by choosing to hang naked on the cross without shame. His entire life portrayed an ethos of love.

John Paul II observes that when Christ calls us to overcome lust in the Sermon on the Mount, His words bear witness that the original grace of creation has become the grace of redemption for each of us.[19] By accepting this redemptive grace and allowing it to transform us, we then allow the third member of the Godhead, the Holy Spirit, to impregnate our sexual desires with the original plan of creation. This frees us from a life dominated by lust and other vices.

As we allow our lusts to be redeemed, we can apply this erotic theology to not only our soul—but to our bodies. This, in turn, allows us the freedom to live out the original sexual meaning of the body, which is a "liberation from lust," which subsequently leads to a consummation with the Spirit.

The Pathos of the Spirit (Consummation)

The word *Pathos* signifies emotion. Further, in rhetoric it is often associated with emotional appeal. In the Pentecostal religion, the Holy Spirit is synonymous with emotion. Speaking in tongues, raising hands, dancing, laughing, and shouting in services are not uncommon. The Pentecostal tradition is known for their emotional music and the "soulish" way they celebrate worship. The worship services can be very sensual in nature.

Almost thirty years ago, I was on a flight to the Midwest, sitting beside a well-known Baptist evangelist. Because he knew I grew up Pentecostal, I was asked the question, "Do you think Pentecostal leaders have a proclivity toward sexual sin?" Now, as a very young and sensitive artist with four generations of Pentecostal leaders as my heritage, not to mention being on the first airplane flight of my life, this question made time seem to literally stand still. It seemed as if everyone on the plane was sitting forward in his or her seat waiting for my answer. Wrestling with the answer led to a passionate and intriguing conversation for the duration of the flight.

There's no denying that the lives of Charismatic leaders who have struggled with sexual sin have been well documented by the media. The excess emotion that characterizes the Pentecostal tradition can indeed lead to a "proclivity" toward sexual sin. However, rather than an indictment on the emotional aspect of ecstatic worship, could it be that this proclivity provides a deeper glimpse into the messiness of a sensual theology?

As one studies religious history, the excesses and failures of leaders seem to always result in overreactions, which in turn lead to new denominations, each with an additional set of rules to "protect" believers from the "sins of the fathers." For example, there is a popular pastor and author from California who has increased his reputation by condemning charismatic denominations and leaders for what he deems their "excesses and errors." This cycle continues and unfortunately, that which God intended to be free and simple (love Him and love others) is rendered controlling and complex (see the Pharisees in Matthew 12 as they condemned the disciples of Jesus who were breaking four of the Pharisees' 39 rules about work on the Sabbath).

But maybe there is another way. Instead of condemnation and judgment that is customarily poured out on Christians by Christians who "fall into sexual sin," maybe we could practice a life of forgiveness and seek to understand that "every knock on the door of a brothel is really a knock at the heart of God." While it may be true that a life lived with excess emotion leads to a proclivity toward sexual sin, the flip side is that this same openness produces a believer who has the potential to more fully understand the mysteries and leading of the Holy Spirit.

The *Catechism* teaches, "Even now (purity of heart) enables us to see according to God...it lets us perceive the human body—ours and our neighbors—as a temple of the Holy Spirit, a manifestation of divine beauty."[20] The Holy Spirit dwells in believers and enables them to live righteous and faithful lives. One nuance of the word consummation is that of completion.

And scripture says, "Through whom (Christ) we have gained access by faith into this grace in which we now stand. We rejoice in the hope of the glory of God...And hope does not disappoint us, because God has poured out his love into our hearts *by the Holy Spirit*, whom he has given us."[21] We can indeed experience a life of hope and completion (of consummation) through the mystery of the Holy Spirit.

God's Original Plan

When we embrace these truths—man's original experiences, fruits of the spirit and body as theology—we will discover God's original plan for our sexuality. Instead of the leering eyes of possessive lust, we will see with Adam's eyes of mutual attraction. Instead of the grasping co-dependency of possessive love, we will relate with patience, gentleness and self-control. And instead of fearing a controlling and judgmental God, we see, in the words of Wesley's classic hymn:

"Jesus, lover of my soul, let me to thy bosom fly,
Other refuge have I none, hangs my helpless soul on thee;
leave, ah! leave me not alone, still support and comfort me!

Thou, O Christ, art all I want; more than all in thee I find:
Plenteous grace with thee is found, grace to cover all my
sin; let the healing streams abound; make and keep me
pure within: thou of life the fountain art, freely let me take
of thee; spring thou up within my heart, rise to all eternity."

For too long, our religious and cultural understanding of sexuality has limited our ability to intimately experience God. To compound that problem, our human capacity for understanding love is limited as well. We are still 100% human. Because of this, we feel uncomfortable with God as our Lover or that He would use our sexuality to lead us to His beauty. The risk feels too great and it exposes the tension between our desire to be loved and fear of rejection.

I believe that a better understanding of the mystery of the Eucharist (also called Holy Communion, or The Lord's Supper) and its multi-layered symbolism may reveal more truth for those of us who desire sacred sexuality. This is not an Agatha Christie mystery we're talking about. It is a glimpse into the transcendent face of God and the essence of our existence.

11.

sex as communion

"Don't tell me there is no mystery."
Bruce Cockburn

As the bedroom door gently closes, we leave behind the outside world and enter another time and space. The room transcends into a mysterious place where the distance that divides us from each other and from God is erased. Lovers enjoying sexual communion become a living expression of the presence of God in His world.

Of course, I should hasten to say there must be a desire for both earthly lovers to enter the room together, not only physically, but spiritually as well. This is exactly why a dualistic philosophy renders the "one flesh" ideal of sex in Ephesians 5 impossible. A *complete* exchange of love in both body and soul is not simply a poetic thought; it is an absolute necessity for the expression of sexual communion.

When we partake in Holy Communion, we meet God in a very direct and intimate way, so sexual communion provides a similar experience. God has created us so that in the mysteries of both, we receive nourishment for both our physical and spiritual needs. We are hungry beings. And we are hungry for God. Behind all the hunger of our life is God and all desire is ultimately a desire for Him.

Because of this, our hunger, and especially our sexual hunger, should be treated with reverence. Sex is a rite. It is an "original sacrament" of intimacy and wholeness, of something much more than raw animal lust. To have sex is much more than maintaining bodily functions; it is the essence of existence. It embodies the original plan of God, when in His first recorded direction to man He calls for propagation. Both Holy Communion and sexual communion provide the opportunity to satisfy that hunger in a mysterious mix of belonging, wholeness, intimacy and transcendence.

Celebrating Holy Communion and sexual communion represents our commitment to God, His commitment to us and our commitment to each other. In their celebration, a transcendence of heaven and earth takes place, and an untouchable God mysteriously touches us corporately and individually in a sacred consummation of holy longing.

Until Christ returns, we have been given two mysterious sacraments as a means to consummate our love for God and each other. In 1 Corinthians, we are told to partake of God's body and blood in Holy Communion until He returns, and in Ephesians 5 we are to partake of our lover's body and soul in Sexual Communion.

Now if you have grown up in the evangelical tradition, much of this may be new to you. Sacraments aren't merely religious rituals as evangelicals are prone to think. They "inject sanctity into the plan of man's humanity and they penetrate the soul and body, both our femininity and masculinity."[1]

The Sacraments make Christ's creation, incarnation, passion, and resurrection a *living reality* in our lives. In the Sacraments, God's love is "poured into our hearts through the holy Spirit."[2] The liturgy and the Holy Eucharist provide incredible power for both our spiritual and sexual relationships, but the church continues to maintain a "don't ask and don't tell" policy about this mysterious and often misunderstood connection.

The Joy of Holy Communion

Holy Communion is a liturgy. In the original meaning of the word, liturgy means an action by which a group of people becomes something corporately which they cannot be as individuals. Liturgy symbolizes a whole greater than the sum of its parts. It is timeless. But Holy Communion is also a sacrament. It is the entrance of the church into the joy of the Lord (Matt. 25:21). This is the essential calling of the Church and its liturgy. The sacrament by which the church "becomes what it is."[3]

Holy Communion can best be understood as a transcendent journey of the Church into the presence of the Lord. To begin this journey, we leave our homes as individuals, male and female, black and white, rich and poor, and come together in one place. In this "coming together," we become a fulfillment of the Church, which is to gather to meet the Lord and to share in His risen life.

The joyful character of the Eucharistic gathering cannot be overemphasized. "The liturgy is, before everything else, the joyous gathering of those who are to meet the risen Lord and to enter with him into the bridal chamber."[4] This joy is expressed in the multi-sensory beauty of the incense, vestments, music, candles, prayers and aesthetics. It is a time of being in the presence of Christ, of a journey to the heavens. And it is a time of mystery.

As we approach the altar, the act signifies that in Christ we have been given access to heaven, and only by grace can we enter and meet the One who is the end of all our hunger and all our desires. This is called the *entrance* of the liturgy, and it symbolizes the next part of the journey from the old into the new.[5]

Through the bread and the wine, we offer all of who we are in a movement of love and adoration to God. Through Christ's death we are given life. Through His life, we are then able to offer our lives to Him and each other by love. We are to be the artwork of God by re-presenting His love.

Transcendent love is at the very heart of the sacrament.

As we prepare to take the bread and the wine into our bodies, we somehow know that it is good to say thanks. Christ is our bread. From the original experience of creation, all our hunger was for Him. His body was transformed into communion with God, and now He shares His body with us. We are offered the bread to help us continually remember that all hunger leads to Him.

Next in our journey comes the high point, the epiclesis, when the Holy Spirit takes us *beyond* ourselves.[6] In scripture, to be "in the Spirit" means to be in heaven. Therefore, it is He who, in an ultimate and mysterious way, makes the transformation of the bread and wine complete. The bread and wine become not mere food, but they symbolize the presence of holy God Himself.

Through this Holy Communion with God (some theologians call it *interpenetration*) not only do we become one body and one soul, but we are restored to that completeness and love the world has lost. We realize that no one is "worthy" to receive communion, but that life comes to us as a free gift. Schmemann says it beautifully: "Adam is again introduced into Paradise, taken out of nothingness and crowned king of creation. Everything is free, nothing is due and yet all is given...There is nothing we can *do*, yet we become all that God wanted us to be from eternity, when we are *eucharistic*."[7]

As we come to the end of this timeless journey, there is an afterglow, an "all is right in the world" feeling that permeates our being. We return to the world in *joy and peace*, completed by the Holy Spirit, having walked in the heavenlies, ready to selflessly share the intimate gift of God's love with others.

This description is not unlike the journey we take with our earthly lover as we prepare to consummate our relationship. It is amazing to see the parallels between the sacred exchange of love in Holy Communion and the joy we find in sexual communion.

The Joy of Sexual Communion

Sexual Communion is also liturgy and a sacrament. It is the entrance of a couple into the profound mystery of the Lord (Eph. 5). This is the essential calling of sexual communion and its liturgy—the sacrament by which the couple "becomes one flesh."[8]

Sexual Communion can best be understood as a transcendent journey of two lovers into the presence of the Lord. To begin this journey, we leave our families and the public world as individuals, male and female, black and white, rich and poor, and come together in one place as a couple. In this "coming together," we become a fulfillment of the Christian life, which is to meet the Lord and to share in His risen life.

Sexual communion should be a transcendent journey and the joyful character of sexual communion cannot be overemphasized. "The liturgy is, before everything else, the joyous gathering of those who are to meet the risen Lord and to enter with him into the bridal chamber."[9] This joy is expressed in the multi-sensory beauty of the atmosphere, lingerie, soft music, candles and aesthetics. It is a time of lovers being in the presence of Christ, of a journey to the heavens. It is also a time of mystery.

An approach to the bed signifies that in Christ we have been given access to heaven, and only by grace can we enter together and meet the One who is the end of all our hunger and all our desires. In true sexual communion, we cannot expect our mate alone to quench all our hunger and fulfill all our desires. Just as in Holy Communion, this *entrance* of the liturgy symbolizes the following part of the journey from public into privacy.

Through a mutual offering of ourselves in sexual foreplay, we offer all of who we are in an erotic movement of love and adoration to each other and to God. Through the mystery of Christ alone we are given full satisfaction. Through His life, we are then able to offer our lives both to Him and to each other in love. We are to be the sensual embodiment of the Church by re-presenting His love. Transcendent sexual love is at the very heart of the sacrament.

It is only by grace that we are able to give selflessly to each other. And as we prepare to take each other into our bodies, to become one flesh, we somehow know that it is good to be thankful for this miraculous and beautiful gift.

Christ is our ultimate satisfaction. From the original experience of creation, all our sexual hunger is for Him. His body was transformed into communion with God, and now He shares His body with us. We share our lover's body to help us continually remember that all our sexual hunger ultimately leads to Him.

Next in our journey comes the high point, the *orgasm,* when the sexual communion takes us *beyond* ourselves. The orgasm represents the most intense physical pleasure mankind can experience. In this most intimate of sexual encounters, we experience a profound unity of body and soul while also recognizing that our partner is "that which is beyond us." Therefore, it is the Holy Spirit, in an ultimate and mysterious way, who makes the transformation of sexual intercourse complete. The orgasm becomes not only incredible pleasure, but also embodies the presence of a God who loves to satisfy our immortal longings.

Through sexual communion (scripture calls it a *profound mystery*) not only do we become one body and one soul, but we are also restored to that completeness and love that fallen man has lost. Sex involves submersing ourselves into the mystery of the other in a pleasurable and exciting act of self-giving and receiving that simultaneously draws us closer to the divine life of the Trinity and each other. To paraphrase Schmemann, "Man and woman are again introduced into Paradise, taken out of nothingness and crowned king of creation. Everything is free, nothing is due and yet all is given....There is nothing we can do, yet we become all that God wanted us to be from eternity, when we are eucharistically sexual."

As we draw to the end of a time of sexual communion, there is an afterglow, an "all is right in the world" feeling that permeates our being. We return to the world in joy and peace, consummated by the Holy Spirit, having walked in the heavenlies, ready to continuously share the intimate gift of God's sexual love with each other.

Celebrating the Mystery

Throughout history, religion has treated human sexuality with a mixture of mystery and control. But selfless and dynamic lovemaking—particularly in the context of marriage—is not only a richly satisfying experience, but also one of the sacramental ways of encountering the mystery we call God (1 John 4:16). The Radio Bible Class teaches that, "Being captured by our lover will give us a taste of being caught up in Christ's love in a way that we feel deeply enjoyed without shame. In essence, sexual communion within marriage should draw us to deeper worship of God who initiated sexuality [both] for His glory [as well as] our delight."[10]

Like the Eucharistic feast called Holy Communion that many Christians celebrate regularly, sexual communion contains amazing parallels and is also a powerful and sacramental celebration of love, both human and divine. God celebrates the mystery of intimate love, and one of the best ways to commune with Him is to be a part of a loving, committed, mutually giving and receiving sexual relationship.

12.

the truth about immortal longings

"I believe in the immortality of the soul because I have within me immortal longings."
Helen Keller

So, what are you hungry for? This is a soulish question. It throbs with the anticipation of a heartfelt answer that encompasses both body and soul. It is not just a physical or sexual question but one that pulsates with spirituality.

Many of us feel the effects of past religious control, and our immortal longings have been rendered shallow and dirty. Many of us have no conceptual knowledge of our beauty because of the legalism and dysfunction of our religion and upbringing. Many of us feel like we're missing something, although we don't quite know what it is. And so we hop from one bed to another, frantically trying to ease our hunger, trying all sorts of sexual fare—Internet pornography, a long-term affair, a quick hook-up with a stranger, sex clubs—in a never-ending search for the perfect mate for our souls. We'd try almost anything to numb the pain of longing and fill the hole we most assuredly feel.

The problem is not that we deny the existence of God, but that we deny His existence in one of the most important aspects of our lives. The wildness of our sexual longings seems entirely too erotic for the sexless God of westernized religion.

Long ago, we learned to view God as an intellectual principle rather than a Lover who longs to romance us. Rarely is there a vital sense of God within our sexual ache. And if it does occur, we feel awkward, ashamed, and embarrassed. In fact, even though most of us believe He created us, we somehow don't think He has any place in our sexuality. God plus sex could not possibly equal fun.

As an impressionable and hormonal young man, I discovered a tattered copy of *The Dairy of Anne Frank* and read this:

> *Today the sun is shining, the sky is a deep blue, there is a lovely breeze and I am longing—so longing for everything. To talk, for freedom, for friends, to be alone.*

> *And I do so long...to cry! I feel as if I am going to burst, and I know it would get better with crying; but I can't, I'm restless, I go from room to room, breathe through the crack of a closed window, feel my heart beating, as if it is saying, "Can you satisfy my longing at last?"*

> *I believe that it is Spring within me, I feel that Spring is awakening, I feel it in my whole body and soul. It is an effort to behave normally. I feel utterly confused. I don't know what to read, what to write, what to do, I only know that I am longing.*[1]

Her words described me and I realized at that moment at least one other person had feelings like mine. As a boy growing up in a deeply religious and culturally isolated family, I was not taught that my sexual longings were "an effort to behave normally." No one ever talked about them at all.

Just like Anne Frank, during the course of our lives, all

of us experience these longings, and unless we understand that God places them within us, they take as their object all sorts of unholy things. We must realize that the quintessential object of our sexual longing is sacred consummation with God. Our mortal longings are simply an effort to behave normally. What a freeing thought!

Mortal Longings

In the sensual longings of our youth, we see a parallel to the garden's original experience of nakedness. We have learned that the nakedness of Adam and Eve in the Garden of Eden portrays a sexual and spiritual mystery. God's plan of love (an emotional biology) calls for the human body to "love as God loves in and through our bodies. And there is no fear (shame) in love."[2] In fact, 1 John 4:18 says that, "perfect love casts out fear." We have been granted the freedom to enjoy unconditional sexuality through the lens of an emotional biology of attraction, pleasure, and procreation.

But when these longings are repressed by false religious teaching, they become distorted. The silence, or worse the "don't do that, it's dirty" mantra of religious lies has resulted in sexual dysfunction.

Adolescents and teenagers must be taught by their parents and religion to understand the reasons for their intense longings. As Pope John Paul II said, "It is an illusion to think we can build a true culture of human life if we do not...accept and experience sexuality and love and the whole of life according to their true meaning and their close inter-connection."[3]

Understanding the true meaning of sexuality and love will result in an awareness of our need for purity. Not perfection—purity. A purity of love. Jesus taught at the Sermon on the Mount that the pure in heart will see God. God originally intended our sexual longings to result in purity. Through a purified awareness, we realize it is not that we are too passionate to walk in love instead of lust, but that we are not passionate enough.

In the soulish longings of adulthood we see a parallel to the Garden's original experience of unity. We long for meaning in life, affirmation, and love, so we frantically pursue the perfect career, the perfect friends, and the perfect children, all at the expense of intimate and unitive relationships with our mate and with God.

When our awareness is purified, through suffering or difficulty, we realize that it is imperative to walk daily in relationship (a communion of persons) with our mate, others, and God, rather than alone. We realize that our sexuality can't be just an emotional biology as it was in our youth; it must also be a *relational spirituality*. Our natural inclination to make it on our own now becomes a supernatural faith in God's original plan for relationship.

The loneliness of Adam in the Garden of Eden reveals God's plan for mankind to "become one flesh," both in marriage and with Him. The original intention of sacred sexuality reveals the spiritual mystery of divine relationship. Scripture provides a beautiful model for life during this season in Galatians 5, which teaches us that the fruit of the Spirit should embody our soul's longings for faithful relationships.

Instead of following the *rules* of religion and culture, we instead pursue relationships in the Spirit. The mystery of the "one flesh" *relationship* of Yada and sacred sexuality in marriage, or as a single adult to God, provides satisfaction for our longings for meaning in life, for affirmation, and for love. This sacred sexuality then embodies our union with God, who is our ultimate soulmate.

In the spiritual longings of an older age, we can see a parallel to the Garden's original experience of solitude. We realize that solitude is not isolation. Instead, the mortal longings for solitude and contemplation prepare us for something more. Instead of succumbing to a natural life of fear and loneliness, our mortal longings transcend to those of a supernatural perception of others, ourselves, and God.

So it is through a selfless love and the encouragement of others that we realize how to best use the freedom of an older age.

During a time of extreme difficulty, I realized the need for the advice of an older, wiser man and so sought someone out for this purpose. Even though I was seeing a trusted counselor, I needed the wisdom of someone who had walked through life and survived. But when I asked this man a very honest question about sexuality, he simply did not have the courage to answer. This was a brilliant man with a vibrant fifty-plus year marriage who was fully alive. I realized then that even though he had a wealth of knowledge, he was afraid and that Satan had somehow tricked him into thinking he had nothing of value to contribute. Another wise man once told me that Satan does not necessarily strive to keep us from the truth; he strives to keep good men (and women) with the truth from each other. This was sadly the case here.

At the risk of over-simplification, in our youth, Satan over-emphasizes eros love (sex without self-sacrificing love) at the expense of agape (self-sacrificing) love. In our middle age, he emphasizes worldly success at the expense of intimate relationships. And in our older age, Satan emphasizes isolation at the expense of legacy. God has placed these mortal longings in us at creation. But Satan has distorted them by offering ever-increasing cravings for ever-diminishing pleasures.

Immortal Longings

The original creation experiences of solitude, unity, and nakedness provide the essence of our immortal longings. These longings call us to participate in God's love and share it with others. When we have the purity to see it, this is what the human body and human sexuality teach us. No wonder Satan tries so hard to corrupt our sexuality.

Second Corinthians 3:17-18 says, "Now the Lord is the Spirit, and where the Spirit of the Lord is, there is freedom. And we, who with unveiled faces all contemplate the Lord's glory, are being transformed into his likeness with ever-increasing glory, which comes from the Lord, who is the Spirit (NIV)." So we see that God, the immortal and ultimate object of our longings, promises unconditional freedom to those who contemplate His glory with unveiled faces. Instead of ever-decreasing pleasure, He promises ever-increasing glory.

We are given the freedom of unconditional sexuality through the miracle of redemption. In a fallen world, we experience lust and control. But in a redeemed world, we experience love and freedom. God does not force us to love, because "forced love is not love at all."[4]

We are free to do what we wish with our sexuality, but we are not free to determine good and evil. While freedom can lead to love, it can also lead to lust. It can lead to faith or it can lead to fear. It can lead to wonder or it can lead to cynicism.

So what if the freedom of sacred sexuality really does embody the essence of life? What if it offers a key—perhaps *the* key—to unlocking the mystery that lies at the heart of our existence, and therefore at the heart of God? If it does, then we who live in an age of religious sexual control need to pay special attention to the freedom God offers us.

The Story of Our Longing

Our story of longing begins in the Garden of Eden and recurs as a constant theme throughout scripture. In the most romantic book of the Bible, Song of Songs, the beloved's heart is compared to an enclosed garden. Then we have the Garden of Gethsemane with Jesus walking through suffering and beyond in order to romance His bride, the Church.

The Bible teaches that our story will end in a Garden, which is located in a new earth. But perhaps the most amazing thing is that while we are waiting for that to happen, God wants to take our body and soul and complete them like He originally planned.

Ever since Man's communion with God was severed in a Garden, we have longed to find this communion again and intimately experience Him. So God is and has always been the object of our longings. Now it finally makes sense that all our longings (sexual and spiritual) intertwine with God's complete intention for our lives.

Redemptive Conversations

For the majority of my life, I had no framework for this extraordinary idea. In my religious circles, sex was what everybody thought about, but nobody talked about.

I hope this book will start conversations. We Americans generally stink at controversial discussions and the subject of sacred sexuality is more than worthy of honest and open debate. Sex is at the heart of almost everything we do as human beings, and if it truly is the essence of existence, then it bears thoughtful and loving consideration among those of us who call ourselves spiritual.

Some people will undoubtedly find portions of this book shocking. Others will think it is tame. It is in no way intended to be a sex manual or a theological treatise. My wish is that it will cause all of us to examine closely our personal longings, our marriages, our relationships, and what we teach our children about sex. Perhaps it's time to utilize the Bible as our sex manual. And for those aspects where it is silent, we should then depend on an open dialogue with those we trust.

My candid conversations with young men I mentor, my own struggles, the shocking results of the online survey, and the inordinate amount of moral dismissals in our churches provided me the incentive to write this book. I have seen wives leave their husbands because of pornography addictions and marriages fall apart due to misplaced affections. Throughout my life, I have seen religion provide judgment instead of grace in almost every situation.

Of course, there are extreme cases of sexual dysfunction that need to be dealt with. Seeing a qualified sex therapist, psychiatrist or licensed marriage counselor is one of the most spiritually mature actions we can take in cases of severe problems.

But I can't help but think that if we really believed our misplaced sexual longings were an indication of a desperate search for God and the original experiences of the Garden, many of us would find redemption instead of condemnation. That's what I've been given. And I'm thankful.

If you get nothing else from this message, know that this book is about redemption. I suppose you could even say it is controversially redemptive. I have realized through the years that it takes shaking up the status quo to get anything accomplished. So be it.

acknowledgments

The creative convergence that has happened "on campus" here in Franklin, TN is reminiscent of a mini-renaissance. While many people consider me to be a Renaissance man, it is only a reflection of the community of friends and confidants surrounding me. Many of them gave selflessly to make this book a reality.

Thanks to those who read countless drafts of this book: Jen Jarnagin, Krissy Thomas, Michele Cushatt, Brandi Wilson, Randy Williams, Keely Scott, and Danny & Betsy DeArmas.

For theological pushback and lively debate on Chapter 1 "Where Soul Meets Body," thanks to Dr. Steve Guthrie. Any theological errors are unequivocally mine.

For crucial input on Chapter 6 "Sexual Equality," thanks goes to Candi Blankman, Nancy Beach, Jenni Catron, and Kari Slusser.

To Matt Maher and Audrey Assad for introducing me to the epic *The Theology of the Body* by Pope John Paul II.

To Ian Morgan Cron for writing *Chasing Francis* and introducing me to Ron Rolheiser's and the contemplative life.

To Dr. Louis Markos, who continues to provide our world with some of the most important academic and accessible Christian thought in modern times.

To my Pastor, Pete Wilson, for his constant support of this book, for his courageous trust to ask me to speak about it at Cross Point, for his warm friendship, and most of all for his grace-filled pastorate.

To my neighbors "on campus," Gail & Mike Hyatt, Karen & Steve Anderson, Patsy & Les Clairmont, Spence Smith, and Matt Brady who have lovingly and kindly discussed the book, and for some reason continue to join me on my back porch for dinner knowing very well the topic of conversation.

The artist-mentoring group that I have led for ten years at Merridees Bakery has endured over two years of conversation about this book. Thanks to Jeremy Thiessen, Brock Gill, Spence Smith, Chad Jarnagin, Randy Williams, David Holloway, Christopher Kemp, and relocated alumni Mark Lee and Glenn Lavender.

To Nordeck & Mary-Claire Thompson for making a big, audacious dream come true at Round Cove. Thanks so much to you both and to Ken & Diane Davis for selflessly giving the sacred space at your cabins, not to mention the extraordinary scenery, where much of this book came to life.

Especially to Karen Anderson throughout the process for her feedback, editing, encouragement, and constant admonition to write like "Pinot Noir" not "Red Bull."

If friends are the family you get to choose, then I have extraordinary relatives. Spence Smith has been a friend, partner, and constant encourager throughout this process.

John Norris, in spite of his thriving cardiology practice, took invaluable time to be my prayer partner and running partner for a decade in Tampa and even though we are separated geographically, he is still one of the three closest friends of my life.

The other two best friends are both named Ken, both live in Franklin, and both share an affinity for a mean game of poker. Both of them have laughed and cried with me through the most crucial times of my life.

Ken Davis is one of the greatest communicators the world has ever known. And one whispered sentence of loving communication to me changed my life forever.

Ken Edwards is my life coach, but more than that, he is my friend. This book is a result of his constant insistence that my longings, all of them, are ultimately for God. When I look into his penetrating blue eyes, I see a loving God.

My editor, Alice Sullivan, has prodded, pushed back, corrected, insisted, commented, deleted, and screamed "eek!" She has provided valuable encouragement and a relentless critique. She is assuredly the most sharp and open-minded person in the publishing industry. If you can comprehend this book at all, it is because of her incredible gifts.

This book is dedicated to my childhood sweetheart, Chris. She has read every draft (and I'm talking hundreds), cooked meals, endured my depression, deleted "Red Bull" writing, worried about what our daughters will think about their Dad writing about sex, then worried about what our parents will think about their son writing about sex. She has been my constant encourager and my lover for over thirty years. Without her, I would not be able to write about sacred sexuality. She has personified Christ to me as no one else in the world. So, a heart-felt toast to the thirteen-year-old blonde, now mother of two extraordinary daughters, and love at first sight and forever.

end credits

Introduction

1. Madonna and Patrick Leonard, "Like A Prayer," Sire Records, 1989, from the album *Like A Prayer*.

Chapter 1: Where Soul Meets Body

1. Peter Brown, *The Body & Society*, Columbia University Press, New York, 2008, p. xviii.
2. Roger Steven Evans, *Sex and Salvation: Virginity as a Soteriological Paradigm in Ancient Christianity*, University Press of America, 2004, retrieved from: http://www.wordtrade.com/religion /christianity/ earlychristianhistoryR.htm on Jan. 13, 2010.
3. John Climacus, *The Ladder*, 15: 889A; p. 177.
4. *Online Etymology Dictionary*. Retrieved January 13, 2010, from Dictionary.com website: http://dictionary.reference.com/browse/ gnostic.
5. Ibid., *The Ladder*, 26:1033D; p. 243.
6. Louis Markos, *Lewis Agonistes*, Broadman & Holman, Nashville, TN.
7. St. Athanasius, *On the Incarnation* (d.373). St. Vladimir's Press. 1977, p. 43.
8. Erwin J. Haeberle, *The Sex Atlas*, Continuum, New York, 1983, p. 3.

Chapter 2: The Lie About Nudity

1. Victoria & Albert Museum website, retrieved Dec. 30, 2009 http:// www.vam.ac.uk/collections/sculpture/stories/david/index.html. In relation to Mr. Dobson's complaint, museum director Caspar Purdon Clarke noted: "The antique casts gallery has been very much used by

private teachers for the instruction of young girl students and none of them has ever complained even indirectly" (museum papers, 1903).
2. Eugene Peterson, *The Message*, NavPress, 2001, Various paraphrases of Song of Songs.
3. Pope John Paul II, *The Theology of the Body*, Pauline Press, Vatican, 63:7.
4. Ibid.

Chapter 3: The Lie About Beauty

1. Patrick Macey, *Bonfire Songs: Savonarola's Musical Legacy* (1998), Clarendon Press, Oxford, pp. 30-31.
2. James Joyce, *The Portrait of The Artist As A Young Man*, Alfred A. Knopf, New York, 1916, pp. 213-215.
3. Ibid.
4. Umberto Eco, *The Aesthetics of Thomas Aquinas*, Harvard University Press, Cambridge, Massachusetts, 1988, pp. 16-17.
5. Pope John Paul II, *The Theology of the Body*, Pauline Books, Vatican, 63:4.
6. Pope John Paul II, Pontifical Address, May 6, 1981.

Chapter 4: The Lie About Self-Pleasure

1. Boyd K. Packer, "To Young Men Only," Lecture at the Mormon General Conference Priesthood Session, October 2, 1976.
2. John C. Dwyer, *Human Sexuality: A Christian View*, Kansas City, MO., Sheed and Ward, 1987, p. 56.
3. Dr. Douglas Rosenau, *A Celebration of Sex*, Nashville, TN, Thomas Nelson, Kindle location 2964-69.
4. *Webster's Revised Unabridged Dictionary*, © 1996, 1998 MICRA, Inc.
5. Alexander Schmemann, *For the Life of the World*, Crestwood, New York, St. Vladimr's Seminary Press, 1973, p. 16.
6. C.S. Lewis, *The Best of C.S. Lewis*, Iverson Associates, New York, 1969, pp. 39-40.
7. Lewis Smedes, *Sex for Christians*, Grand Rapids, Eerdmans, 1976, p. 163.
8. Ibid., A Celebration of Sex, Kindle location, 3068-73.
9. Ibid., Kindle location, 1167-72.
10. Ibid., Kindle location, 2957-62.
11. Mark A. Michaels and Patricia Johnson, *The Essence of Tantric Sexuality*, Woodbury, MN, Llewellyn, 2006, p. 69.
12. Robert Burns, *Poems and Songs*, The Harvard Classics, 1909-14.
13. Ibid., *For the Life of the World*, p. 16.

Chapter 5: The Lie About Sexual Fantasy

1. http://www.merriam-webster.com/dictionary/masochism and http://www.merriam-webster.com/dictionary/sadism.
2. Dr. Douglas Rosenau, *A Celebration of Sex*, Nashville, TN, Thomas Nelson, Kindle location 1861-67.
3. Ibid., location 1974-78.
4. Barry W. and Emily McCarthy, *Discovering Your Couple Sexual Style*, New York, NY, Routledge, 2009, pp. 59-60.
5. Kevin Leman, *Sheet Music, Uncovering the Secrets of Sexual Intimacy in Marriage*, Wheaton, Illinois, Tyndale House, 2003, p. 238.
6. Wendell Berry, *Standing By Words*, San Francisco, CA, North Point Press, 1983, p. 90.

Chapter 6: The Lie About Sexual Equality

1. Manning and Zuckerman, *Sex & Religion*, Thomson Wadsworth, Belmont, CA, 2005, p. 127.
2. Mary Stewart Van Leeuwans, *Gender and Grace*.
3. Baptist Faith and Message, section XVIII, "The Family," retrieved Dec. 29, 2009, from http://sbc.net/bfm/bfm2000.asp.
4. Bartky, Sandra Lee, *Femininity and Domination: Studies in the Phenomenology of Oppression* (Routledge, 1990), p. 26.
5. Ward, L.M. (2002). Does television exposure affect emerging adults' attitudes and assumptions about sexual relationships? Correlational and experimental confirmation. *Journal of Youth & Adolescence*, 31, 1–15.
6. Dr. Louis Markos, from his personal writings, Houston, TX.
7. American Psychological Association, "Task Force on the Sexualization of Girls" (2007). Report of the APA Task Force on the Sexualization of Girls. Washington, DC: American Psychological Association. Retrieved from www.apa.org/pi/wpo/sexualization.html.
8. Satcher, 2001; Sexuality Information and Education Council of the United States [SIECUS], 2004.
9. Fredrickson, B. L., & Roberts, T. A. (1997). "Objectification theory: Toward understanding women's lived experience and mental health risks." *Psychology of Women Quarterly*, 21, pp. 173-206.
10. Grauerholz, E., & King, A. (1997). Primetime sexual harassment. Violence Against Women, 3, pp. 129-148.
11. Ibid., Does television exposure affect emerging adults' attitudes and assumptions about sexual relationships? Correlational and

experimental confirmation. *Journal of Youth & Adolescence*, 31, 1–15.

12. Greenberg, B. S., Siemicki, M., Dorfman, S., Heeter, C., Stanley, C., Soderman, A., & Linsangan, R. (1993). Sex content in R-rated films viewed by adolescents. In B. S. Greenberg, J. D. Brown, & N. Buerkel-Rothfuss (Eds.), *Media, Sex, and the Adolescent* (pp. 45-58). Cresskill, NJ: Hampton Press.

13. Kelly, J., & Smith, S. L. (2006). "Where the girls aren't: Gender disparity saturates G-rated films" [Research brief]. Retrieved August 31, 2006, from www.thriveoncreative.com/clients/seejane/pdfs/where.the.girls.arent.pdf.

14. Duffy, M., & Gotcher, J.M. (1996). Crucial advice on how to get the guy: The rhetorical vision of power and seduction in the teen magazine YM. *Journal of Communication Inquiry*, 20, pp. 32-48.

15. Fink, J .S., & Kensicki, L. J. (2002). "An imperceptible difference: Visual and textual constructions of femininity in *Sports Illustrated* and *Sports Illustrated for Women*." *Mass Communication & Society*, 5, pp. 317-339.

16. Merskin, D. (2004). "Reviving Lolita? A media literacy examination of sexual portrayals of girls in fashion advertising." *American Behavioral Scientist*, 48, pp. 119-129.

17. Slater, A., & Tiggemann, M. (2002). "A test of objectification theory in adolescent girls." *Sex Roles*, 46, pp. 343-349.

18. Madeline L'Engle, *Walking on Water*, Crosswicks, Wheaton, Ill, 1980, p. 36.

Chapter 7: The Lie About Yada, Yada, Yada

1. Retrieved from http://www.ancient-hebrew.org/emagazine/018.html on Jan. 16, 2009.

2. "But now he has reconciled you by Christ's physical body through death to present you holy in his sight, without blemish and free from accusation."

3. Eph. 2:6: "And God raised us up with Christ and seated us with him in the heavenly realms in Christ Jesus."

4. Louis Markos, From an unpublished paper, Houston, TX.

5. Retrieved from http://www.everything.com/The-Body-Erogenous-Zones/ by Suzie Heumann & Susan Campbell, Ph.D.

6. See Chapter 8, "An Emotional Biology," for further explanation on pheromones. For a detailed study of these fascinating olfactory chemical messages, see the study conducted by Professor Martha McClintock, which is widely available on the Internet.

7. Dr. Kevin Leman, *Sheet Music*, Wheaton, IL, Tyndale, 2003, pp. 112-113.

8. John Donne, "Holy Sonnet," *Poems of John Donne*, Vol. I, E.K. Chambers, ed., London, Lawrence & Bullen, 1896, p. 165.

Chapter 8: Sacred Sexuality (An Emotional Biology)

1. The Pontifical Council for the Family.
2. "Individual and Gender Fingerprints in Human Body Odour," by Karl Grammer, http://www.pubmedcentral.nih.gov/articlerender. fcgi?artid=2359862. Published by The Royal Society.
3. C.S. Lewis, *The Best of C.S. Lewis*, Iverson Associates, New York, 1969, pp. 39-40.
4. Piccinino, L.J., Mosher, W.D. "Trends in contraceptive method use in the United States: 1982-1994." 1998. *Family Planning Perspectives.* Vol. 30(1): 4-10 & 6, Table 1.
5. Pinkerton, S.D., Bogart, L.M., Cecil, H., & Abramson, P.R. (2002). "Factors associated with masturbation in a collegiate sample." *Journal of Psychology and Human Sexuality*, Vol. 14(2/3), pp. 103-121.
6. Laumann, E., Gagnon, J.H., Michael, R.T., and Michaels, S. *The Social Organization of Sexuality: Sexual Practices in the United States.* 1994. Chicago: University of Chicago Press (Also reported in the companion volume, Michael et al, *Sex in America: A Definitive Survey*, 1994).
7. Read more at www.suite101: Plan a Babymoon Vacation: Babymoon Vacation Trip Planning, http://familytravel.suite101.com/article.cfm/ planababymoonvacation#ixzzocobCIzID.
8. Psalm 127:5.
9. Psalm 127:3.
10. Christopher West, "Theology of the Body for Beginners," 2004 Ascension Press, p. 9.
11. A catechism, in its most basic sense, is a set of questions and answers used to explain a larger topic. Normally, though, catechism refers specifically to a summary of religious doctrine, used for religious instruction and to answer questions of faith and morality. Think of it as a religion's textbook. "What is the Catechism?" 24 Nov 2009, http://www.cliffsnotes.com/WileyCDA/Section/id-305403,articleId-63923.html.
12. *American Heritage Dictionary of the English Language.*

Chapter 9: Sacred Sexuality (A Relational Spirituality)

1. Second Vatican Council, Gaudium et spes, no. 24, in *Vatican Council II, Volume 1: The Counciar and Postconciliar Documents*, ed. Austin Flannery, O.P. new rev. ed., Northport, NY, Costello, 1992.
2. C.S. Lewis, *Surprised By Joy*, p. 28.
3. Christopher West, *Theology of the Body for Beginners*, West Chester, PA, Ascension Press, 2004, p. 29.
4. John 15:4.
5. Psalm 51:12.

6. Gailliot MT, Baumeister RF, "The Physiology of Willpower: linking blood glucose to self-control." _Journal of Personality and Social Psychology_, Rev 11 (4), 2007, pp. 303–27.

Chapter 10: Sacred Sexuality (A Theology of the Body)

1. Pope John Paul II, _The Theology of the Body: Human Love In The Divine Plan_, Pauline Press, 1980.
2. St. Athanasius, _On the Incarnation_.
3. Pope John Paul II, _Theology of the Body: Human Love In The Divine Plan_, Pauline Press.
4. Ibid.
5. Dr. Louis Markos, "Two Shall Become One," Excerpted from a chapter from an upcoming book.
6. Christopher West, _Theology of the Body for Beginners_, West Chester, PA, Ascension Press, 2004, p. 5.
7. Ibid., _Theology of the Body: Human Love In The Divine Plan_.
8. Genesis 2:18.
9. Genesis 2:18.
10. Genesis 2:23.
11. Ibid., 11.2.
12. Ibid., 11.3.
13. Ibid., 11.3.
14. Ibid., 13.1.
15. Ibid., 19.1.
16. Sermon 69, c.2,3, St. Augustine.
17. Max Weber, _Essays in Sociology_, New York, Oxford University Press, 1946, p. 323.
18. Eugene Peterson, _The Message_, John 1:14.
19. Ibid., Theology of the Body: Human Love In The Divine Plan.
20. CCC. N. 2519.
21. Romans 5:1-5.

Chapter 11: Sex As Communion

1. Alexander Schmemann, _For the Life of The World_, p. 26. 1973 St. Vladimr's Seminary Press.
2. Ibid., p. 29.
3. Romano Guardini, _The church and the Catholic, and the Spirit of the Liturgy_ (New York, 1950), pp. 180-181.
4. Alexander Schmemann, _For the Life of The World_, Crestwood, NY, St. Vladimir's Seminary Press, 1973, p. 45.
5. Ibid., p. 31.
6. Ibid., p. 39.

7. Ibid., p. 43.
8. Christopher West, *Theology of the Body for Beginners*, West Chester, PA, Ascension Press, 2004, p. 5.
9. Ibid., *For the Life of The World*, p. 26.
10. Radio Bible Class, "What's the Purpose of Sex?" from the RBC website:http://www.gospelcom.net/rbc/questions/answer.php?catagory=ethics&folder=sex&topic=Sex&file=purpose.xml.

Chapter 12: Immortal Longings

1. Anne Frank, *The Dairy of A Young Girl*, New York: Doubleday, 1967, p. 134.
2. Pope John Paul II, *The Gospel of Life*, n.97.
3. Christopher West, *Theology of the Body for Beginners*, West Chester, PA, Ascension Press, 2004, pp. 14-15.
4. Ibid.

Breinigsville, PA USA
04 February 2010
231958BV00002B/2/P